Gender on Wall Street

Laura Mattia

Gender on Wall Street

Uncovering Opportunities for Women
in Financial Services

Laura Mattia
Muma College of Business
University of South Florida
Tampa, FL, USA

ISBN 978-3-319-75549-6   ISBN 978-3-319-75550-2   (eBook)
https://doi.org/10.1007/978-3-319-75550-2

Library of Congress Control Number: 2018934629

Cover credit: Spencer Platt/Staff/Getty Images
Cover design: Ran Shauli

Printed on acid-free paper

This Palgrave Macmillan imprint is published by the registered company
Springer International Publishing AG part of Springer Nature
The registered company address is: Gewerbestrasse 11, 6330 Cham, Switzerland

To my daughters Alexandra and Leamarie whose STAR power
inspires and motivates me.
And to my husband, Mark, for his everlasting support
and my sons Christopher and Kyle for their encouragement.
I am forever grateful.

CONTENTS

Part III   The STAR Plan

List of Figures

CHAPTER 1

Introduction

This book is about creating your story, which starts by answering the following question: What do I choose to do next? Many people struggle in life until they realize that life, on its own, has no inherent meaning. We give our lives meaning by the vision that we set, the choices we make, the obstacles we overcome, and the rewards we reap through our experiences.

Often though, we hold onto experiences or expectations that get in the way of the life we're trying to create. We interpret certain situations in a way that makes us angry or anxious, which can affect our behavior and our potential for success. Those negative interactions can damage our self-confidence to the degree that we feel compelled to give up. Part of creating your story comes from knowing what is relevant and important to you and the reality of what it takes to be in charge of your own life. I was able to create a story which inspires me, and my hope is that you will be able to create your own inspirational story. It starts by:

- Understanding that negative experiences or people you encounter have nothing to do with you. Don't hold onto the negativity and don't internalize it.
- Whatever happened is the past (even if it happened five minutes ago). Embrace the fact that you get to decide what's next.
- Choose a path that supports your personal values and vision for your life and your career. Your values are the foundation of a strategic career plan.

This book is organized into three sections to help you effectively become a female financial star by developing:

1. A vision of your life and career which focuses on the opportunity for women in financial services.

© The Author(s) 2018
L. Mattia, *Gender on Wall Street*,
https://doi.org/10.1007/978-3-319-75550-2_1

2. An awareness and understanding of gender-specific challenges so you can avoid or reduce threats to your career goals.
3. A strategic mind-set using the STAR process to create a personal career plan.

Why do I think this is important enough to write about it? I've been there. I've struggled in the trenches of the financial world—as a woman—to build a career and a reputation for myself. I've seen what goes on and how people treat each other. In response to workplace realities, I've developed a winning formula for success because I want to see other women succeed.

LIFE ON MARS

Growing up with artists for parents, my family never had money. I started working full time at sixteen. Somehow, I convinced my high school to let me leave at 12:30 every day so I could work an eight-hour shift at Sears. Although Sears offered a management track in lieu of college, I declined. Instead, I chose college and worked as a cocktail waitress/bartender to pay for my tuition.

After graduating with a degree in psychology, I worked for People Express Airlines as a customer service manager and was promoted to team leader. Before graduating from business school, I had already worked for thirteen years full time where hard work was appreciated and the idea of meritocracy was reinforced.

Because of my prior work experience, I was not prepared for what happened next, upon graduating from business school with an MBA. I was hired as a cost accounting manager at M&M/Mars in the Hackettstown, NJ plant. Everyone told me how hard it was to get into the company and how fortunate I was. The recruiter said that even though it was a large company, the staff was treated like family.

Employees were expected to work hard but they were highly compensated, and the benefits were beyond what most companies offered in 1990. The company maintained a generous defined benefit plan that guaranteed income in retirement. The overall compensation package created a competitive workforce, which was made up of people from all over the world. Many people inside the "family" were proud to call themselves "Martians."

I didn't just enter an international manufacturing/marketing behemoth; I entered a position in finance within that environment. I soon learned the position was just as coveted as a position at Goldman Sachs or any of the major New York firms. Many finance professionals made the conscious decision to work at Mars over Wall Street.

On my first day, I arrived early and immediately went to get changed. We had to wear whites because we spent time on the manufacturing floor. As a cost accountant, it was my job to understand the manufacturing process and how it drove the cost of the product.

When I walked into the plant office, Dana, a woman I met during the interview process approached me. Although she was informative in the interview, it was clear she was not my biggest fan. I felt sure I could win her over quickly and planned to focus on trying. I wasn't prepared for what came out of her mouth though. Her exact words were, "Why are you here? I told Richard not to hire you." I remember it as if it were yesterday because I was shocked.

This set the stage for a rocky relationship made worse by the fact that Dana was supposed to train me and help me with my responsibilities. Her idea of training was to yell at me. For example, instead of telling me to prepare a document called a "Scrap Report," she stood in the middle of the office and yelled, "Why didn't you complete the Scrap Report? What is wrong with you? You are incompetent!" No one at Mars had an office, regardless of what part of the company you worked for. Everyone sat in one big room. At headquarters, the room was the size of a stadium but you could see clearly from one side of the room to the next. If someone yelled loud enough, you could hear them as well.

With no policy or procedure manual in place, Dana continued to berate me in public. She spoke badly about me to all of the other managers in the plant office, most of whom were male. There were very few (if any) other female managers. Dana was an exception. Her treatment toward me established the initial response and lack of cooperation that I received from the plant workers those first three months. She attacked my competence and my confidence suffered, but within a few months, I learned what was required of me and turned it around.

I began to streamline the monthly processes and make improvements. One of the first things I did was create a policy and procedure manual so the next person wouldn't have to deal with Dana. I maintained my composure (there is no crying in baseball … or at work) and got the job done, which helped me to earn the respect of the plant workers. Their confidence served me well to fix long-standing problems, which made everyone's job easier.

From our initial introduction, Dana's strong reaction to me indicated some form of discrimination. Enough was said about female incompetence throughout the training ordeal that it became clear my gender was a problem and the intention was to exploit this stereotype. Female on female bullying is a gender-specific problem not legally protected even though the goal is to intimidate, demoralize, and destroy career potential. Dana liked her queen bee status in the Hackettstown plant and didn't want me, or anyone else, to encroach on it. I needed a strategy to divert her efforts.

Instead of allowing her insults to affect me, I rejected her crude assessment and focused on what I was hired to do. *I quickly established* my credibility to obviate her damaging accusations. Dana did not know me. She concluded who I was and what I was capable of based upon *a* judgment. Her insecurity and generalizations had nothing to do with me. This was not my problem—it was hers and I refused to own it. Some women never reach their potential because of someone else's inaccurate assessment or ulterior motives but only you really know what you are capable of. Trust your instincts and let your actions dictate the story.

THE NUMBERS DON'T LIE

Gender-specific challenges exist in all financial roles whether internal to other industries or in the financial services industry, serving the economic needs of individuals, businesses, and nonprofit organizations. While the financial organizations recognize the need to reduce direct and indirect discrimination of women in financial roles, the intention of this book is to empower the women themselves to influence change while using tools to ensure success. The industry needs help because it has been posited that women require a critical mass in the executive ranks (30%) in order to have direct influence over organizations. Forecasts based upon current rates of change do not project this goal will be met until the middle of this century.[1] That is too long to wait.

Today, 23% of Certified Financial Planners (CFP®s) and 16% of Chartered Financial Analysts (CFA®s) in America are women. Both are considered gold standard designations in the financial services industry. The percentages of women with financial designations are misleading because not everyone who obtained these designations is working in the finance industry. Some are academics, some have chosen not to work, and others have left the industry out of frustration.

Drilling down further to identify the percentage of women working in financial services, I explored data sets used in recent research. The biggest challenge in isolating exactly how many women work in financial services (in non-support or non-clerical roles) is that there is no universal definition of "financial advisor or planner." Most of the research uses data sets where females make up between 10 and 15% of the "financial advisor" population. In the studies where advisors traded investment instruments, as investment managers or fund managers, the percentage of women in those data sets drops below 10%. Women involved in fund management tend to manage passive portfolios versus active portfolios. Active management offers higher compensation, increased status, and they are the more coveted positions. Passive management positions are not mission-critical and are more likely to be eliminated through automation and robo-advisor offerings. Further, qualified females report working in support roles rather than critical investment or client facing roles, which affects their status, compensation, and job fulfillment.[2]

[1] Joecks, J., Pull, K., & Vetter, K. (2013). Gender diversity in the boardroom and firm performance: What exactly constitutes a "critical mass?". *Journal of Business Ethics, 118*(1), 61–72.

[2] http://www.CFAinstitute.org/wim.

Culture usually emanates from the top. One of the reasons there are not more women financial advisors could be related to the leadership at the top in the financial services industry. Again, financial services include a broad range of business models. In the banking sector, a 2014 analysis by the *New York Times* examined the percentage of women serving on senior management committees at five of the major banks. Women made up to half of the employees at these firms, but clearly that number is not reflected in the percentage of female leadership.

- Citigroup: 4%
- Goldman Sachs: 13%
- Morgan Stanley: 13%
- JPMorgan Chase: 17%
- Bank of America: 36%.[3]

Research by Mercer, a consultancy, who conducted a large online survey of females working in the financial services industry across the USA found the proportion of women diminishes as one moves up the corporate ladder at the financial services firms.[4] Mercer's study showed that while 71% of the support staff are women, 40% of the managers and 21% of the executives are women. The study also showed that a lower percentage of women are hired into the upper ranks than men, a lower percentage of women are promoted to the next level than men, and a higher percentage of women than men exit the organization even once they have been promoted to higher levels.

Although the 1960s women's movement happened almost sixty years ago and women have made enormous strides in gender equality working in many occupations historically occupied by males, social norms continue to restrict progress. Actually, the women's movement is considered to have occurred in four waves, which began in the early 20th century and although each wave had its own focus, the issues always included women's ability to influence, equality, fair treatment and economic concerns.[5]

1. Early 20th Century focused on legal and social equality and the right to vote,
2. The 1960s focused on political and social equality and women's liberation,
3. The 1990s focused on the intersectional nature of identity and difficulties juggling career and motherhood, and
4. In 2012 the focus turned to an opposition of sexual harrassment, violence against women and women's role as world stewards.

[3] http://www.financial-planning.com/news/yellens-impact-on-banking-glass-ceiling.

[4] http://www.oliverwyman.com/content/dam/oliver-wyman/global/en/2016/june/WiFS/WomenInFinancialServices_2016.pdf.

[5] Wrye, H. K. (2009). The fourth wave of feminism: Psychoanalytic perspectives introductory remarks. *Studies in Gender and Sexuality, 10*(4), 185–189.

Despite rapid progress in many industries from 1970 through 1990, economists show that progress has slowed in recent years and the research numbers don't lie. I advocate for a fifth wave now, where women focus on areas with clear power inequality, starting with the financial sector and women's relationship with money, which is where ultimate power resides.

MONEY IS POWER

Female mastery of money, one of the major sources of power in the world, is the final key to balancing equity among the genders. The reason I am passionate about encouraging women in the financial services sector is because only when we achieve a balanced gender representation all the way up the ranks, will we be on equal footing.

Understanding, managing, controlling, earning, and spending money confer status, privilege, power, and freedom—and control of everyone and everything that money can buy or influence. When women acquire financial skills and knowledge, they can tip the scales of gender-linked power in their direction. This is a key reason why it's so important for women to become financial leaders and advisors, so they can encourage other women to become financially engaged.

Financial abilities go beyond successful employment; they allow women to live their lives on their own terms instead of someone else's. This is true freedom, which allows you to avoid or leave destructive or unhealthy relationships. It gives you the confidence and security to enjoy your life with less uncertainty.

The finance industry's male-dominated tradition is long established, which makes it difficult for women to succeed. (Some of the challenges for women within the financial services environment are highlighted in this book.) The financial industry was created before women participated in financial matters and consisted of men advising men, who tend to approach money differently than women.

Historically, the finance industry has:

- Employed risky investment strategies focused on short-term wins over long-term sustainability.
- Tended to focus on sales objectives to grow profits for the company instead of counseling and advising objectives that improve client's lives.
- Assumed that women were not interested or capable of understanding, deeming explanations a waste of time. This prevents discussion that can create partnerships to engage participation.

The societal tradition of female non-participation in financial discussions is not effective. Things have changed. Women need to participate to survive; to earn a living; to be empowered; and to provide for themselves and their families. Although there are many organizations committed to fix the situation, women themselves need to rise up and help fix it. Women cannot sit back and wait for everything to fall in place. They have the power to create change.

If we simply commit to achieving critical mass in the finance industry, the situation will take care of itself. Whether you work in a corporate financial department, an investment bank, a venture capitalist group, an investment firm, or a wealth management firm, there is one thing these jobs have in common: control of money.

Financial services offer a unique situation where money and human ideals collide. This is the sweet spot. With the tools for conscious engagement, women can be inspired, motivated, and successful.

What You Will Find in This Book

Anecdotal Stories

To identify potential hurdles so that you can effectively navigate your career, I use personal stories, stories I have heard from other women I've mentored or who have confided in me, and stories from well-known women that have been shared in public forums. Although not all my experiences are in financial services, they have been in financial positions that exposed limitations for women in finance. I left out last names to protect privacy and in some cases changed the first name.

Empirical Evidence

In addition to industry studies, I use empirical studies to support some of my observations. The scientific process has always appealed to me because it goes beyond anecdotal and singular experiences, analyzing large data sets of many experiences, which can be generalized (within limitations). Surveys that do not apply the rigor of science are interesting but, at best, show raw trends or differences where there may be a perfectly good explanation. Multiple regression performed on large data sets is a statistical technique that controls for all possible explanations, which highlight unexplained differences.

These techniques are used to identify the direct effect and the interactions of possible explanatory variables on the outcome (in this instance, the difference between how males and females experience financial services careers or differences between females in financial services and females in other industries). These techniques are very powerful and indisputable, although I am certain you can find exceptions to the findings. In statistical terms, the exceptions are called outliers since they stand-alone and are not part of the trend. Although interesting, outliers cannot be generalized and don't provide insight regarding shared experiences. Scientific studies that show statistical significance cannot be overlooked since they help prepare you for possibilities that have been experienced by many women and therefore empower your strategy.

Mentor Insight

Without role models, a personal mentor, or coach, it can be hard to discern how to handle a sticky situation. Mentor Insights are peppered throughout the book to provide ideas on how to think about or handle certain situations. Everyone's experiences are unique, so the Mentor Insights are intended to get you thinking about how to address similar situations.

Exercises for Conscious Engagement to Create Your STAR Career Plan

Conscious engagement is the act of mindfully creating your own work experience. It is a method of choosing how you participate and stick to a strategy designed to take you where you want to go. To get the most out of this book, the exercises will help you develop your personal STAR career plan. Planning charts a course for the achievement of your vision. The exercises will guide you through the critical process of allocating your resources, time, and energy to develop thought patterns that will make you a financial services STAR.

The STAR Career Plan

This book focuses on how you experience your career as a woman. It will teach you how to control what is within your power to control. To achieve a successful career in financial services, you need to maximize your resources by following the STAR formula:

- Strategic Framework—Create a vision for your Brand (avert gender-specific challenges).
- Technical Skills—Fortify your Brand (leave no room for doubt).
- Advocacy Circle—Develop your Brand (leverage the bigger mind).
- Relationships—Share your Brand (win over partners and advocates).

Your plan must start with conscious engagement, which is all about focusing on what you need to do to become a female financial services STAR. Just like a plan that you develop for your clients, your personal STAR plan must be disciplined. It must consider the big picture prize, which includes your vision for your life and your career. It must also recognize the gender-specific challenges that have the potential to divert your plan. You need to be aware of these challenges without giving them power. You do that by focusing on your STAR career plan. Choose conscience engagement; you will find the rewards are well worth it.

Disclaimer: I am not anti-men, and I don't support women who are. I don't blame men for the current situation.

I truly hope the men (the brave and the curious) who read this book are able to see that I am not tearing them down or berating them for the current situation in the workplace. It is not the fault of men that women did not historically participate in finance. Why would men create an environment to support women if there were no women there to support?

PART I

The Opportunity for Women

CHAPTER 2

The Rewards of a Career in Finance

Erin is a 29-year-old financial planner. She is facing her first set of gender-related setbacks. Erin is concerned she's not on partner track due to her inability to comfortably socialize with her male superiors at bars and on the golf course. She also recently became aware that the administrative staff projected their girlfriends' or mothers' "nagging" onto her when she gives them instructions or follows up on client progress. In her annual review, she noticed that she and the other female financial planner in the firm were more harshly criticized than their male peers for the firm's shortcomings.

Erin sailed through school, often told by her professors and parents that she "could do anything she put her mind to." But now, she stays awake nights wondering, "Is it me? What am I doing wrong?" Erin was thrilled when she got her first job in finance right out of college, but now she is starting to doubt her chosen profession and her ability to climb the ladder. She's thinking about returning to graduate school for a master's in education, even though a teaching career won't satisfy her financial and overall career goals.

When Erin and I met, she had all but given notice to her firm. She lived in Flemington, N.J., which is a few hours from where I lived. She had seen me on Channel 12 and listened to my podcasts. Erin said I seemed approachable because I taught at Rutgers University and did a lot of outreach. She was ready to give up, and what I found so frustrating was that she thought she had failed.

When we got together, she told me about the recent annual review she received from her boss. The focus was on the new business she had brought in over the past year. Erin was particularly proud of the work she had done with one of her newer clients, Barbara, whom she knew really appreciated her work. In fact, as a thank you for helping to get her financial life in order, Barbara invited Erin to the New York Symphony Orchestra at Lincoln Center where she played the clarinet.

© The Author(s) 2018
L. Mattia, *Gender on Wall Street*,
https://doi.org/10.1007/978-3-319-75550-2_2

13

Barbara needed the help. When her father passed away, she received a $13-million-dollar inheritance. She had no idea how to protect it, grow it, or how to take an income stream out of the portfolio that would last throughout her life. Erin created a financial plan for Barbara that included a long-term investment strategy for all of her assets plus a substrategy for the $5-million-dollar portfolio Barbara gave Erin to manage.

Barbara did not turn over her entire portfolio because she had never worked with a financial advisor and was scared. Erin understood the need for patience and felt that over time, as they developed a stronger relationship, she would eventually receive more of the assets to manage.

Her boss didn't see it the same way. Instead of congratulating her for the account, which was sizeable, he focused on the $8M Erin did not directly manage. Immediately, he began comparing her performance to others in the firm. He said, "Robert (the top producer) would have been much more aggressive to make sure all the assets came to us." Although Erin did not say it, we both knew that Barbara would never have met with Robert, and even if she did, she would have run from his aggressive pursuit of her assets.

Erin was demoralized. She said every performance review over the past five years had been just as bad. "At first," she lamented, "I thought it was just a learning curve and I would eventually show my worth, but now it doesn't seem like I will ever show my worth. I guess I'm just not good at this. Funny though, I really like my clients and they seem to like me too. I know I make a difference in their lives."

Erin and I discussed her situation further, and we talked about what attracted her to the financial services industry to begin with. She always wanted to go into a helping profession but also wanted it to be practical. She told me a story about her mother who divorced her father and never seemed to have enough money. Her mother made many bad financial decisions. She lost a lot of money working with a financial advisor who was not a fiduciary who had convinced her to put all her money into a private hedge fund. The fund failed in 2008, and all of Erin's mother's savings were gone.

Erin couldn't believe her mother had been taken advantage of like that. She wanted to help other women make responsible financial decisions to improve their lives. As we talked, I saw how alive Erin became as she described the work she did for her clients.

There was nothing wrong with Erin. (If I still owned my wealth management firm, I would hire her in a heartbeat.) She needed to make some decisions. First, she needed to define what she needed from a financial firm to be (and feel) successful. Then, she needed to evaluate if she could reposition herself. Was it possible to change her relationship with her boss, her peers, and the administrative staff at her current firm, or did she need to go to a new firm to start fresh with a clear strategy?

Erin was tempted to leave the industry altogether, as she had shared with me, but the rewards of working in financial services are too great to give up. Ultimately, she decided to remain in finance because the profession was aligned with her values and the work inspired her. It's a field that offers opportunity to make a real difference in people's lives, as Erin had done for Barbara. If Barbara's sizeable inheritance fell into the wrong hands, she could have quickly wound up broke like Erin's mother.

Mentor Insight: A career in financial services can satisfy many needs, but if the work is not aligned with your values, you will quickly become disengaged and ultimately, unsuccessful. Many people end up in a career for the wrong reasons. Your values define what is important to you and what motivates you. They should guide your career decisions from the outset.

Your engagement at work—in terms of effort, commitment, and motivation—is directly related to how well your career fits with your values. Your personal values are what give your career purpose. They should be the primary reason for choosing a career in finance, which offers multiple rewards that satisfy a range of values. For example:

- You might choose a job as a financial advisor for a Women's Center because you value **altruism** and **community**, wanting to make a difference in women's lives.
- Or you might enjoy working for a large, well-known banking conglomerate because you value **prestige** and **large financial rewards**.
- Or maybe you would prefer to set up your own practice because you value **independence** and **flexibility**.
- Or maybe you prefer a partnership with a couple of other financial advisors because you value **team membership** and **security**.

VALUES BEYOND MONEY

When I first went to college at the age of 17, I majored in psychology and dance, hoping to work with autistic children through a field called Dance Therapy. I was encouraged to go this direction by my parents, who were both artists. I was brought up to have a low regard for anything business related, especially finance because, according to my parents, people in finance didn't create anything and did not add value to society.

My parents were good people. They had strong morals and wide-ranging knowledge, but they weren't right about everything. On the topic of business, I later learned they were dead wrong. Initially, I pursued the MBA for monetary reasons and survival—I had a baby and, without getting into the details of my financial struggles, I decided I needed a good paying job to feed and provide for my son. Yet once immersed in the coursework, I began to understand how and why capitalism works for the betterment of the whole, not just for the powerful.

I learned how wealth is created and driven by the private sector to optimize resources. Financial institutions create and manage the process of effectively using our resources to improve the quality of our lives. Financial people make this system work using information and judgment. They help move money through the system as a tool to better society.

Although financial intermediaries have always impacted society, recently a term called "social finance" has emerged, which is a means to explicitly unite profit, social and environmental aspects to positively impact business and society. The international forum of governments and central banks in the top twenty countries (the G20 or Group of Twenty) encourage financial institutions to support the world's small and medium-sized enterprises (SMEs) so that people are pulled out of poverty and economic stability strengthens communities.[1] Millennials and financial institutions themselves are beginning to recognize how financial institutions can directly make a difference in the quality of our lives.

In fact, many students I've worked with through my years as a professor have been inspired by finance for reasons beyond money. Certainly, they expect to be compensated but they also believe in personal responsibility combined with the ability to positively influence other people's lives.

Surveys confirm careers in financial services as one of the highest in job satisfaction. The industry and the people it serves are desperate for good financial thinking, which allows exposure to many new and interesting people and opportunities. Working as a financial advisor can be particularly fulfilling because you have the opportunity to help individuals and families find solutions to meet their financial goals and to live better lives.

I will never forget the first time a group of clients showered me with hugs and kisses and told me how fortunate they were to have found my firm. It was the summer of 2008, which was the height of the recession, and we were at a town hall meeting I had orchestrated. It was a difficult time for everyone. My partners were against the idea of hosting the meeting. They thought people would be throwing tomatoes at us, but I insisted. Difficult periods are when our clients need us the most, and I was right.

The clients were grateful that we showed leadership to explain our decisions and articulate our plan. Everyone was scared; they needed to understand what was going on; and they wanted the truth. We felt good about the work we had done because we protected them from the huge losses of the market. (They were down but only by half that of the market.) To receive such unconditional, affectionate feedback made me smile all over. The financial advisor role helps people make decisions that impact their lives, their families, and society as a whole. There is strong gratification in knowing you have helped someone fulfill their dreams and protect their nest egg.

In addition, the connection you make with people can be profound. You have the opportunity to build lasting, meaningful friendships for life. I can't help but care about my clients; I want them to be successful and happy and they know it. In my mind, everything else pales in comparison. It fuels my number one work value, which is to influence lives. In fact, my goal is to transform lives by helping people set themselves on a new trajectory toward

[1] https://www.changemakers.com/g20media/socialfinance.

achieving their goals and dreams. And I have done that by helping people use money as a tool (not as the end goal) to live out their vision—incidentally what I hope to inspire in you, the reader of this book.

Financial services offer challenging work that requires critical thinking and problem-solving skills, which contribute to your overall satisfaction. There are diverse ways to utilize these skills and various types of organizations. From striking out on your own (the Bureau of Labor Statistics identified nearly 1 in 4 personal financial planners were self-employed in 2016), to working at firms big or small, the jobs pay well and are satisfying. For millennials who want a career with a purpose, financial advising delivers.

You determine where and how you work. Do you want to work from home, from a large office, for a big conglomerate, or in a small office? Where in the country do you want to work? Complexities of the markets and the dynamic sociopolitical environments can take you all over the world. A well-thought-out business plan can make international placement possible. There are financial service professionals who work from their boat or on the beach. You determine what works best for you, your values, and your relationships.

If you're in the right business model, you can determine when you work in addition to where you work. This is an occupation where face time is not absolutely necessary for success. As long as you get the job done, it doesn't matter when you do it. Of course, some organizations burden their employees with unproductive requirements to consistently show up, but if flexibility is one of your priorities, there are plenty of organizations that allow it and will work around your schedule.

Flexibility tends to be important criteria for women who have children or other family obligations. A good portion of financial service professionals are entrepreneurs or independent contractors who are aligned with larger companies but work from home. Some go into the office several times a week and work from home the other days. It's a job you can make work for you.

According to the *Bureau of Labor Statistics Occupational Handbook*, personal financial advising is expected to be one of the fastest growing occupations, right along healthcare jobs. The changing demographics in America and the aging population means that people require financial guidance to protect and grow wealth, as well as create an income stream during retirement.

In-demand occupations translate to job security, which allows you the freedom to switch organizations if your firm does not provide you with the right type of support. There are growing possibilities in an evolving profession where new opportunities arise to satisfy household demand. The demand will continue as new and creative technologies and work-processes continue to be developed.

A career in financial services provides opportunity for continuous education and growth. It is intellectually stimulating and by the nature of the work, there are always new things to learn. This is not a job where you will watch the clock or become bored. There are many opportunities for continuing education, whether it be another degree, certification, or simply researching a new topic.

As a finance professional, people are interested in what you know, which generates conversation and discussions. Networking is an important part of the profession; people are generally interested in financial matters so financial professionals command a level of respect and status. It's widely recognized that financial services careers require intellect, education, and hard work; therefore, others will seek your perspective and opinion. You could find yourself at the center of conversations if you are up to date on the latest financial news. Even at parties, people are hungry to hear an intelligent market assessment that is not tied to someone trying to sell or market a product or idea. People respect responsible judgment.

It is also important to recognize that financial services skills are transferable and highly sought after in related professions. Interpersonal skills, technical skills, critical thinking, and judgment are necessary components in many job descriptions. For example, Certified Financial Planners—a gold standard in the financial services industry—are taught to look at the whole picture and then to explore all the different options. The new practice *Standards for the Financial Planning Process* outlines seven-steps to analyze an individual's current situation and determine how they can use financial resources to meet goals. This process is intuitive and supports good decision making, even basic thought processes like planning for a trip. The ability to go through a robust decision-making process methodically is one of the most important leadership skills required in the workplace (Fig. 2.1).

Mentor Insight: Talents well suited for a career in finance include analytical and critical thinking skills, good judgment, self-discipline, patience in delaying gratification, the ability to see the bigger picture, understanding consequences, a penchant for fairness, perseverance, trustworthiness, and honesty.

Fig. 2.1   The financial planning and decision making processes

Exercise: Analyzing Your Career Values

People who choose a financial services career will have different values but also are often inspired by similar values such as achievement and helping people.

Why This Career?

Who made the decision that you would pursue your career? Did *you* decide, did you fall into it, or did someone else push you toward it? The more your choice was based on your personal preferences and values, the more likely you will be happy in your career.

_____

_____

_____

_____

_____

_____

_____

_____

What did you know about the financial services industry before you decided to enter into the industry?

_____

_____

_____

_____

_____

_____

_____

What attracted you to the industry?

_____

_____

_____

_____

_____

_____

_____

What is Important?

Ask yourself, what is most important to me? Am I meeting my needs or do I see a path to eventually meet those needs?

– Career First: Some people believe you should first choose the career and then find the business model that suits your lifestyle.
– Lifestyle First: Others say you should approach your career understanding how you want to live your life and then choose a career that fits your lifestyle.

Pick five of the values listed below that are the most important to you and the five that are least important to you.

- FAMILY: Provide adequate time for me to spend with my family.
- HEALTH: Allow time for exercise, eating well, and mindfulness.
- EDUCATION: The opportunity to receive formal and informal training and development.
- FRIENDSHIPS: The ability to curate new friends and maintain old friends.
- PHILANTHROPY: Engage in activities (financially and/or time) to give back.
- MATERIAL BENEFITS: The financial or other material rewards that ensure a comfortable lifestyle.
- BALANCE: Allow time for family and leisure.
- AESTHETICS: The appreciation of beauty.
- COMMUNITY: Involvement in politics, service projects, or volunteering.
- INDEPENDENCE: The freedom to work alone, make your own decisions, and plan your own work.
- FLEXIBILITY: The ability to work at different places and times.
- LARGE FINANCIAL REWARD: Earnings above-average income.
- COMPETENCE: The ability to demonstrate a high degree of expertise and mastery of skills.
- KNOWLEDGE/RESEARCH: Engaged in the pursuit of knowledge and truth.
- INFLUENCING PEOPLE: Involved in influencing opinions and behaviors of other people.
- PEOPLE CONTACT: Enjoy the connection with other people.
- RESPONSIBILITY: Demonstrate trustworthiness and reliability.
- MORAL/SPIRITUAL: Live out ideals or moral code.
- RECOGNITION: Receive positive feedback and acknowledgment of good work.
- INTELLECTUAL CHALLENGE: Keep the mind active and constantly thinking.
- ACCOMPLISHMENT: Set goals and achieving them.
- CURIOSITY: The opportunity to explore new ideas.
- ALTRUISM: Help and advise others for the greater good.

- ADVENTURE/RISK-TAKING: The sense of excitement, adventure, and challenge that comes from taking risks, either personal, social, or physical.
- VARIETY: Change and diversity in work content, personal contacts, or location.
- PRESTIGE: The status, recognition, and importance of your profession, the firm that you are associated with, or with your own accomplishments.
- LEADERSHIP: Provide direction and instruction to others to achieve a common goal.
- TEAM MEMBERSHIP: Work in close cooperation with others to achieve a common goal.
- ADVANCEMENT: Promotion, career progression, and ability to get ahead rapidly.
- SECURITY: Stability of employment and assured salary.
- CREATIVITY: Create new ways of working or new services to offer clients.
- OTHER: Other values associated with work.

Write the five most important and the five least important values below. On a scale of 1–5 (1 being not at all satisfied in your current job and 5 being highly satisfied in your current job), rank which values are being satisfied. Evaluate how well your current job fits your important values and not your least important values.

Most important	Rating	Least important	Rating
_____	___	_____	___
_____	___	_____	___
_____	___	_____	___
_____	___	_____	___

Reflect on your answers above. Are your values reflected within your work or does something need to change? What can you change so that your work is better aligned with your values?

_____
_____
_____
_____
_____
_____
_____
_____
_____
_____

What if you knew for a fact that you would be successful in any job you pursued in the financial services industry? What type of business (or what type of firm) would you work for? Where would the business be located? What would your job title be? What would a day in that job look like?

_____

_____

_____

_____

_____

_____

_____

_____

_____

_____

_____

_____

_____

CHAPTER 3

The Win for Financial Services

Laila's fee-only firm was struggling before she was hired. Unlike many other fee-only firms, this one had only accumulated $40 million dollars in assets under management (AUM), in sixteen years. Laila, a CFP® and MBA, knew the firm had had difficulties and conflicts with business partners and false starts in the past. She also knew they lacked several crucial skills.

First, no one at the firm was a CFP®, nor did they really understand the elements of a financial plan. The firm received 100% of their prospects from family and friends and the National Association of Personal Financial Planners' (NAPFA's) lead generation Web site.

Although they were grandfathered into NAPFA, Laila knew the affiliation was a conflict because clients assumed NAPFA firms had certain competency skills, which her partners did not have.

Second, no one was equipped with marketing knowledge to promote the firm. Third, no one participated in networking or business development activities. In fact, no one worked to cultivate the relationships they had with their small but loyal client base. All of the weaknesses were Laila's strengths, and she knew she could help the team.

Laila was comforted by the fact that the three partners wanted to do the right thing for their clients. Hiring her was an indication of their intent. They were also skilled in doing the parts of the job that Laila didn't care to do. Michael knew what was required to run a small business because his family owned a restaurant. John, took care of the nitty-gritty details such as compliance and billing documents. Tom, who had been a market maker on the NYC Stock Exchange trading floor, executed all of the trades.

Laila had been in business development at a marketing company. At her new firm, she created marketing programs focused on specialized niches, attended various networking groups, developed educational programs to reach new prospects, developed relationships with television and other media outlets to appear on programs, and created outreach programs to better

© The Author(s) 2018
L. Mattia, *Gender on Wall Street*,
https://doi.org/10.1007/978-3-319-75550-2_3

connect with clients. She also brought in alternative ways of servicing clients such as working on bifurcated trusts for special needs families and using directed IRAs to invest in start-up businesses and real estate. These additional techniques were new for the partners, and they welcomed her expertise.

Laila also attracted a following of women who liked her empathetic, patient style. She did not speak down to them, and she explained financial concepts in simple terms they understood. When Laila recognized that her partners did not have the tolerance to properly serve some of the less confident clients, she picked up the phone to check in. She brought unique skills, characteristics, and fresh ideas to grow the business. They were a more diverse group because of her, and she balanced out the characteristics and skills of her male counterparts. This resulted in an organic 20% compounded annual growth rate (CAGR) due to new clients over an eight-year period—well beyond what the firm achieved prior to Laila joining.

Mentor Insight: Research shows gender diversification goes beyond contributing just social benefits but also contributes economic benefits due to diversification of thought, abilities and characteristics. Despite growing evidence, there is a still a lack of individual and institutional awareness of these material advantages.

THE IMPACT OF GENDER DIVERSITY: BETTER RESULTS

The financial services industry is in desperate need of professional women. Women bring diverse perspectives that are instrumental to business and allow for a new level of innovative ideas. Even small ideas can have a major impact on the business, the industry, the economy, and society. There is an opportunity to make a big difference, not just for the clients served, but for the wider community as well.

Laila demonstrated there is a strong business case for gender diversity in financial services. Numerous studies have also shown that gender and racially diverse firms tend to perform better than those without diversity. They are more successful in attracting top talent and improving their customer orientation, employee satisfaction, and overall decision-making capability, which results in increased returns.

This starts at the top. Advocates of diversity in corporate governance—the process by which companies are directed and controlled—believe there is a direct correlation between board diversity and shareholder value. There is much evidence to support the belief. David Carter, Betty Simkins, and Gary Simpson, from Oklahoma State University, analyzed Fortune 1000 companies, looking at size, industry, and other corporate governance measures. They found a significant positive relationship between the percentage of women or minorities on the board and the value of the firm.[1]

[1] Carter, D. A., Simkins, B. J., & Simpson, W. G. (2003). Corporate governance, board diversity, and firm value. *Financial Review, 38*(1), 33–53.

Other studies have shown that public companies with one or more women on the board achieve a higher return on equity than those that don't have women on the board, and mixed investment teams slightly outperform single-gender teams.[2] Theresa Welbourne, from the University of Michigan, with Cynthia Cycyota and Claudia Ferrante from the US Air Force Academy, analyzed 534 IPO firms and found that firms with women in senior positions achieved higher short-term financial metrics such as the Tobin's Q (market price to book value per share), three-year stock price growth, and growth in earnings per share.[3] Just like Laila's contribution to the firm, they attribute the positive effect of the senior women, due to diverse ideas that bring on better innovation and problem solving. Numerous additional studies throughout the world have produced similar findings.

On the other hand, a lack of diversity at the top results in a less integrated workforce: fertile ground for conflict, an ineffective workforce, and poor overall performance. These factors contribute to difficulties with retention, high absenteeism, and low engagement—all of which increase operating costs and decrease profitability.

Overall, financial decision making has been shown to improve with diversity, from running operations to selecting investments. Gender balance creates excess returns, what we call alpha in the investment world, which just like investing comes from disparate ideas that generate new solutions and innovation. When investing, we recognize that alpha represents the value a portfolio manager adds or subtracts from a fund's returns. In the financial firm, incremental returns can be attributed to a more distinct expertise from a new and less correlated source—a woman.

Women add a new dimension to the industry, potentially improving the profession's image and sustaining its future. A more diverse talent pool provides better services for customers and supports a stronger economy. Beyond the benefits to the operations of the business, female financial advisors are thought to have unique listening, communication, and caring skills that make them particularly adept at capturing revenue. As the industry moves toward behaving more as fiduciaries, who put the client's interest first, and less as salespeople, who conduct transactions, these innate skills will become even more valuable.

While many people appreciate the skills that women possess, female advisors can theoretically attract the women of households to participate in the financial decision making. This action alone could improve consumer financial behavior and financial well-being and positively affect the entire economy.

---

[2] CS Gemder 3000 Women in Senior Management, September 2014, Fund Managers by Gender, Morningstar, June 2015.

[3] Welbourne, T. M., Cycyota, C. S., & Ferrante, C. J. (2007). Wall street reaction to women in IPOs: An examination of gender diversity in top management teams. *Group & Organization Management, 32*(5), 524–547.

And the time is right. There is a confluence of circumstances and demographics, which makes this particular time in our history appropriate for women to choose leadership positions in financial roles. Historically, men have held those positions, and they range from working in the corporate sector to working with individuals in financial services.

Working in financial services is particularly attractive due to the direct influence on people's lives, but there are other financial careers to consider. Titles don't always reflect the actual work because universal definitions for many financial positions don't exist.

Nevertheless, all financial organizations—and even financial departments within other industry sectors—experience a shortage in female professionals. The opportunity and necessity for gender diversity is upon us now. Just a few of the many opportunities for women, where diversity can improve organizational return, include:

- CFO or controller
- Corporate advisor
- Financial analyst
- Investment banker
- Sell side analyst
- Mutual fund analyst
- Hedge fund manager
- Venture capital analyst
- Private equity expert
- Mutual fund analyst
- Financial advisor
- Wealth manager
- Investment manager
- Personal financial planner/advisor

EDUCATION VS. RESISTANCE

In the past, women didn't choose finance degrees; so naturally, there wasn't a large supply of financially well-educated women. Today, pundits suggest that women are rectifying this restriction since they are receiving bachelor degrees in greater numbers than men. Yet they still don't choose to study finance, financial planning, or even pursue advanced certifications. The percent of women with financial designations has not increased in over a decade.

Women are beginning to recognize the benefits of pursuing a career in personal financial planning. According to a 2017 study done by TD Ameritrade, 36% of financial planning students today are women.[4] Compare that

---

[4] https://www.financial-planning.com/slideshow/td-ameritrade-on-program-directors-of-financial-planning-college-programs?brief=00000153-6773-d15a-abd7-efff45d10000.

percentage to the fact that 56% of American college undergraduates are women and 50% of medical students,[5] 47.0% of J.D. students,[6] and over 50% of accounting students[7] are women. Many finance-bound students may also look to pursue an MBA. Even there, women account for only 40% of the students at the top MBA programs.[8] This percentage has risen rapidly as more women decide to prepare themselves for the business world. Considering, however, that more women than men receive their undergraduate degrees, and women are nearing 50% in the fields of law and medicine at the graduate level, business schools have been slower to catch up.

The education statistics partially explain why there are not more professional, upper level women in financial service firms. The industry is aware that finance is not an obvious career choice for women and has begun to actively recruit women to the industry. This is certainly a step forward, but there still are numerous hurdles.

Harvard University economist, Claudia Goldin, argues that men underestimate women's skills based on female underrepresentation in the industry, which they see as a sign that women are less productive and capable.[9] Lack of women in finance triggers a negative stereotype about women's inability to perform in finance. Creating circular reasoning on par to the chicken or egg debate, this mentality results in fewer women being hired, which only reinforces the underrepresentation.[10]

From the male perspective, Goldin identifies a concern that allowing more women into the field would signal a negative change in financial profession standards. Many other STEM studies have shown similar stereotyping.[11] In the investment world, where overconfident investment managers believe they are able to beat the market despite statistical probability, the perceived inferior status of female investors spoils the illusion of predicting the markets. Goldin suggests females pollute the male illusion of status. However, when women are able to prove competence with the appropriate education and credentials, this concern is diminished. Goldin's research emphasizes the need

---

[5] https://blogs.wsj.com/experts/2015/10/29/the-good-and-bad-statistics-on-women-in-medicine/.

[6] American Bar Association, "Enrollment and degrees awarded 1963–2012."

[7] National Center for Education Statistics, "Table 318.30. Bachelor's, master's, and doctor's degrees conferred by postsecondary institutions, by sex of student and discipline division: 2012–13," Digest of Education Statistics (2013).

[8] http://fortune.com/2015/11/09/women-mba-40-percent/.

[9] Goldin, C. (2014). A grand gender convergence: Its last chapter. *The American Economic Review, 104*(4), 1091–1119.

[10] Goldin, C. (2014). A pollution theory of discrimination: Male and female differences in occupations and earnings. In *Human capital in history: The American record* (pp. 313–348). University of Chicago Press.

[11] For example, STEM majors; Cheryan, S., Ziegler, S. A., Montoya, A. K., & Jiang, L. (2017). Why are some STEM fields more gender balanced than others? *Psychological Bulletin, 143*(1), 1; Riegle-Crumb, C., & Morton, K. (2017). Gendered expectations: Examining how peers shape female students' intent to pursue STEM fields. *Frontiers in Psychology, 8*, 329;

for women to be technically educated and hold credentials to validate admission into the high-status finance profession.

Mentor Insight: Technical competence is the single biggest differentiator in the financial services industry. It sends a signal of competence. See Chapter 11 for further discussion.

An alternative explanation on why women are not hired was proposed by Nobel Prize winning economist, George Akerlof, from Georgetown University, and Rachel Kranston an economist from Duke University. They used game theory to identify male discrimination against women. Akerlof and Kranston assert that men don't discriminate against women because of inferior capabilities; it's just about power in the workplace. They posited that women threaten the finance profession's masculine reputation. Men want to protect the social power of the "the boys club."[12]

Given its history, finance is viewed as a competitive occupation incongruent with female's stereotypes associated with helping and working with others, so it turns some women off. Psychological studies have shown that men are more competitive than women and take more risks. These gender differences can explain why more women don't pursue financial careers.

In a recent study, Muriel Niederle from Stanford University and Lise Vesterlund from the University of Pittsburgh examined women and men who work under a non-competitive task where they were simply paid by the work completed as opposed to a competitive compensation model.[13] The researchers measured and compared the participant's preferences. The results indicated that equally able men and women differ substantially in competitive preferences. While women shy away from rivalry, men were drawn to it. The researchers also showed that high performing women avoided the competitive choice even though they were most likely to excel, while low performing men selected it, even though they were more likely to fail.

This desire to avoid competition has been observed in situations described as "win-lose" exchanges. Since some women view working in a male-dominated career such as finance as a "win-lose" proposition, the desire to avoid competition can explain why women reject finance as a career.[14] Interestingly, this can also explain why women circumvent negotiations, shy away from sales positions, and avoid potentially confrontational situations. In the end,

Inzlicht, M., & Ben-Zeev, T. (2000). A threatening intellectual environment: Why females are susceptible to experiencing problem-solving deficits in the presence of males. *Psychological Science, 11*(5), 365–371; Murphy, M. C., Steele, C. M., & Gross, J. J. (2007). Signaling threat: How situational cues affect women in math, science, and engineering settings. *Psychological Science, 18*(10), 879–885; Sekaquaptewa, D., & Thompson, M. (2003). Solo status, stereotype threat, and performance expectancies: Their effects on women's performance. *Journal of Experimental Social Psychology, 39*(1), 68–74.

[12]Akerlof, G. A., & Kranton, R. E. (2000). Economics and identity. *The Quarterly Journal of Economics, 115*(3), 715–753.

[13]Niederle, M., & Vesterlund, L. (2007). Do women shy away from competition? Do men compete too much? *The Quarterly Journal of Economics, 122*(3), 1067–1101.

[14]Babcock, L., Laschever, S., Gelfand, M., & Small, D. (2003). Nice girls don't ask. *Harvard Business Review, 81*(10).

the decision to avoid a career in financial service may have less to do with ability, concern about discrimination, or the desire for a work–life balance than a lack of propensity toward choosing a competitive career.

Mentor Insight: Although financial services historically had been a competitive industry, the profession is rapidly changing and clients are demanding more responsible counseling in their best interest. Savvy clients are seeking collaborative advisors who educate and counsel them. Current and future advisors will be successful if they focus on client needs and not on their own agenda to win. The financial services occupation is in transition—transforming for the better.

TIME FOR INCLUSION

Generally, women are thought to be more communicative, supportive, and empathetic than men. These characteristics have the potential to put women at a comparative advantage in business, particularly in client facing financial positions where the goal is to become a trusted advisor and work in the client's best interest.

However, we need to be cautious and advise people not to take the idea of female comparative advantage too far. Several counterproductive articles have been written that exaggerate women's dominant leadership abilities, which has had an adverse affect.[15, 16, 17]

Joris Lammers and Anne Gast from the University of Cologne, Germany explore the sensational media claims that forecast female advancement as a superpower and identify the harm it creates.[18] Lammers and Gast discovered through a series of experiments that people are less inclined to support women's success in the workplace when they read articles about females destined to be the primary financial leaders. Certainly, these types of claims would not make anyone, particularly a male who might feel vulnerable, compelled to help the cause. Conversely, when female strengths were discussed without hyperbole and belittlement of their male counterparts, the same negative effect did not occur.

I have seen firsthand how concerns related to a change in female financial leadership status can create anxiety. I was speaking at a Wealth Management Summit about the benefits of including women as valuable partners in financial services businesses. The owner of a wealth management firm operating as

[15] Sharpe, R. (2000, November 20). As leaders, women rule: New studies find that female managers outshine their male counterparts in almost every measure. *Businessweek*, p. 74. Retrieved December 15, 2000, from *Businessweek* Online, http://www.businessweek.com/commonframes/ca.htm?/2000/0047/b3708145.htm.

[16] Heffernan, M. (2002, August). The female CEO ca. 2002. *Fast Company*, 61, 9, 58, 60, 62, 64, 66.

[17] Conlin, M. (2003, May 26). The new gender gap: From kindergarten to grad school, boys are becoming the second sex. *Businessweek*. Retrieved September 18, 2006, from http://www.businessweek.com/magazine/content/0321/b3834001mz001.htm?chan=search.

[18] Lammers, J., & Gast, A. (2017). Stressing the advantages of female leadership can place women at a disadvantage. *Social Psychology*.

a registered investment advisor (RIA) approached me at the end of my talk. He was obviously agitated. He started by saying, "What is wrong with you women?" (Not the most professional introduction.) He hadn't heard a word I said. Instead of looking at women as a potential contributor to his firm's success, he saw the prospect of including women as a scarcity problem; their success would be his demise. He had so completely dug in his heals with a preconceived opinion that he could not envision the positive outcome and the benefit to his firm.

The encounter reminded me of an article I wrote for ABC.com a few years ago, "How Women Can Keep from Making Themselves Victim in Divorce."[19] The article discussed the need for women to take control of their future. They should not depend on an ex-husband to help them become financially stable. My goal was to encourage women to plan for their future, instead of relying on the false magic of alimony, and to stand up on their own two feet.

I expected a negative reaction to the article from women, but all of the angry emails I received were from men. Rather than acknowledging the practicality and benefits of women becoming independent and empowered, the emails called women bloodsuckers and said I was encouraging them to complain and whine.

Female financial independence can be a threatening proposition to some men, but it helps all members of the family, especially the children, if the wife/mother is able to provide for the household. I'm not sure the men who responded to my article even bothered to read it, and if so, they were so entrenched in their own story of how things work; they couldn't get past their anger to see the wisdom of the advice.

Fortunately, I did receive some positive feedback from women who agreed they needed to take action. I even received a few male comments that said the advice was refreshing. However, the episode at the conference and the reaction to my article demonstrates why we need to be honest and foster open dialogue.

In her book, *Lean In*, Sheryl Saunders shares a story about going to a business meeting in NYC. She asked where she could find the "ladies room" and was told they didn't have one. The reason they didn't have a ladies room was because there were never any women in the office. That makes sense and no one can blame the owners of the firm for not creating something that wasn't needed. Now that women are starting to come to the office, we're asking that someone install a ladies room and a few of the other necessities we need to be successful. Fortunately, the financial services industry is making an effort to do just that.

[19] http://abcnews.go.com/Business/women-making-victims-divorce/story?id=25235357.

The Need for Female Financial Advisors

There is an urgent need for the financial services industry to attract, hire, train, and retain qualified female advisors/planners over the next several decades. The urgency is due to the vast wealth transfer underway in America, as well as technological advances in the delivery of services. Every financial services firm faces the challenge of building and maintaining the infrastructure necessary to provide value-added service and advice.

According the Occupational Outlook Handbook produced by the Bureau of Labor, the need for financial advisors is expected to grow by 15% through 2026. Compare that figure to the need for accounting professionals, which is expected to grow by 10%. The average growth rate for all other professions is 7%.

The financial services industry needs to look for creative ways to attract advisors (and fast). Firms that create friendly environments for female advisors by providing opportunities for recognition, growth, equal pay, and flexibility will have a competitive advantage. Consider the following:

- Today most people plan to retire without pension plans. Where in the past, employers took responsibility for ensuring an income stream, retirees are now left to figure out how to protect, grow and take an income stream from their retirement savings. With baby boomers retiring, demand for financial advisors is on the rise.
- The average financial advisor in the USA is in his or her mid-50s and is considering retirement. More than 10,000 advisors and planners are expected to retire annually in the coming years. Nearly 1/3 of all planners and advisors currently working will be retired in 10 years.[20]
- Less than 5% of financial advisors and planners are under the age of 30, and only 20% are under the age of 40.

The talent shortage is reminiscent of the situation created by the bull market in the summer of 1982 when Wall Street was desperate for talent. Many women got their entree into the financial field during that time, but the trend did not continue. It even began to unravel as the industry succumbed to aggressive behaviors in the late 1980s and 1990s, which resulted in numerous crises including the long-term capital collapse, currency issues, the tech bubble, the great recession, and many other legal and ethical blemishes on the financial services industry.

Yet, the climate is different this time. Consumers are looking for responsible behavior from Wall Street, and they want fiduciaries to advise them. Being the "winner" or beating the market is no longer in vogue. Instead, people want someone to help them make good financial decisions that protect their wealth and improve their family's well-being.

[20] https://www.cfp.net/news-events/research-facts-figures/cfp-professional-demographics.

Women are also better prepared today than they were a few decades ago. Instead of being victims of the system, they can help to structure the system in a way that is better for the economy and for everyone. The financial services profession is evolving from a highly competitive industry to one that focuses on service and meeting consumer needs.

WOMEN AND WEALTH

While the demand for financial advisors/planners continues to grow, we need to take a closer look at where the demand is coming from. Historically, financial decision making has been done by single men, single women, and married men but not married women. But married women are now engaging in financial decision making. According to an industry study, only 14% of married women in 2006 were involved in financial decision making, but by 2014, eight years later, 27% of married women were involved in financial decision making.[21]

Women are recognizing that they will most likely be responsible for financial decisions at some point due to divorce or the fact that they have a longer life expectancy than men. Additionally, as more women become high earners, they want to ensure their hard earned money is properly managed. Yet, according to research done by the Center for Talent Innovation (CTI), over half of the women earning $100,000 a year or more, or who possess investable assets of at least half a million dollars, don't work with a financial advisor.[22] Participating in financial decision making does not necessary equate to comfort with the financial services industry.

Women simply don't approach money in the same way as men. They tend to look for trusted relationships where their financial advisor understands their needs. Some women acknowledge they prefer to work with a female advisor but more are agnostic of gender. Most women don't want to be told what to do or respond to the, "don't worry about it, I know best" attitude that is common in the industry. Women want to develop an understanding of their options through conversation and explanations. They want to be included in the problem-solving process, and they want to collaborate on the right solutions to feel secure.

Kathleen Burns Kingsbury, a wealth psychology expert, outlined the differences in how to communicate with women in her book, *How to Give Financial Advice to Women*.[23] She highlights the need for women to be included in the discussion through a collaborative process, connecting and working with others to achieve financial security (Fig. 3.1).

---

[21] http://www.prudential.com/media/managed/wm/media/Pru_Women_Study_2014.pdf.

[22] https://hbr.org/2014/12/the-financial-services-industrys-untapped-market.

[23] Kingsbury, K. B. (2013). *How to give financial advice to couples: Essential skills for balancing high-net-worth clients' needs.* McGraw Hill Professional.

Fig. 3.1 Key gender differences (*Source* Kingsbury, Kathleen Burns. How to give financial advice to women: Attracting and retaining high-net-worth female clients. New York: The McGraw-Hill Companies, 2013. Print)

It is expected that women will control over $22 trillion in wealth by 2020. The industry is starting to recognize that influential women are looking for financial advisors who know how to communicate with them. Female advisors are uniquely equipped to understand the financial needs of their peers and can easily partner with this sector of the market. While Kathleen Burns Kingsbury focuses on the female client, it is also important to acknowledge the female advisor also tends to communicate in a more participatory, collaborative manner—not just for the female client but also for sophisticated male clients who are looking for responsible guidance through a partnership.

As a wealth manager who specializes in working with women, men have sought me out for the unique skills that I offer in terms of communication, partnering, and understanding what wealth means to them. They have told me they know that women are held to a higher standard in finance than their male colleagues, so successful women will tend to be superiorly skilled. This truism has been a major advantage for me to attract clients, and again, it highlights the importance of technical competence and the opportunity that exists for all female advisors.

Our recent research into women in finance led me to data collected from the Economics of Loyalty Study, where I used a data set that included 1229 respondents from the USA and 753 respondents from the UK. We performed regression analysis to control for extraneous variables and evaluate how female and male clients develop satisfaction with and loyalty to their female or male advisors.

We found female clients placed higher importance on most financial service skills than male clients. Female clients tended to lean on obvious signs of customer service and benevolence to evaluate their advisor rather than technical competence (likely due to their inability to evaluate technical skills). Although many women indicated a preference to work with a female advisor, they rated their male adviser higher than their female advisor in most skills, particularly technical skill. I was surprised by these results since it appears that women are more critical of female advisors than male advisors.

People tend to evaluate an advisor's performance based on emotional stereotypes associated with how they classify the advisor. As a financial advisor (and a woman), I know people use shortcuts and heuristics in decision making. If the only differentiation between two advisors is their gender, this becomes the relevant classification.

Women who have participated in traditional gender roles throughout their lives may be even more emotionally committed to gender biases than males. Many women develop beliefs about inferior mathematical ability at a young age. I see this in the classroom all the time where young women believe they are incapable of math. Female coworkers and subordinates often react negatively to women violating gender stereotypes and can be more critical of females working in traditional male roles.[24]

The finance industry is evolving quickly and striving to help women become more successful. There are many organizations that are actively working toward greater equality in the financial services sector, but it's hard to change a mind-set and a culture that was built over thousands of years. While they try to pull women up, female financial professionals also need do some heavy lifting. We have a responsibility to ensure our own success.

[24] Parks-Stamm, E. J., Heilman, M. E., & Hearns, K. A. (2008). Motivated to penalize: Women's strategic rejection of successful women. *Personality and Social Psychology Bulletin, 34*(2), 237–247.

Exercise: Identifying and Utilizing Your Strengths

When I studied psychology in the early 1980s, the emphasis was on what was *wrong* with you. I didn't find this helpful because I don't think people should focus on history or negative experiences. The behavioral psychologist, Abraham Maslow, turned the tide and started to examine the idea of creating what positively motivates individuals. His motivational theory was built upon a hierarchy of needs for achievement where self-actualization is the highest level. Achieving self-actualization occurs when one realizes their personal potential and achieves self-fulfillment.

In 1988, a new field of psychology emerged from the work of Dr. Martin Seligman. His premise was that psychologists had very little scientific knowledge about how to build people's well-being. Where traditional psychology focused on what was wrong with people, Seligman's positive psychology studied what is *right* with people. In other words, positive psychology is the science of how to promote well-being and self-confidence.

The concept of "learned helplessness" was also being explored at the time. Based on animal research, it examined how subjects avoided negative stimulus and relinquished control over their lives and how those behaviors were linked to depression. Martin Seligman, a researcher involved in the learned helplessness movement, began to study how children could be taught to look at events optimistically using cognitive behavioral exercises.

Seligman's research led to the development of a scientific theory on how to create happiness. He found that the most satisfied and optimistic people were those who understood their personal strengths. By developing and using those strengths in every situation possible, they were able to create a well-lived and fulfilling life.[25] The emphasis of this approach is self-awareness.

Scientists have found that every person has a unique constellation of 24 character strengths that cross cultures, nations, and religions. Greater awareness and use of character strengths are associated with increased goal achievement, improved health and happiness, and stronger relationships.

Researchers in positive psychology developed a questionnaire that measures and provides language for your strengths. It's called the VIA—Values in Action—questionnaire.[26] The survey can be found at http://www.viacharacter.org. Hundreds of thousands of people have taken this questionnaire; there are 120 questions, which take approximately 20 minutes to complete. The survey gives you the rank order of your strengths for free, but if you want a more detailed report, it can be purchased for $20.

---

[25] Seligman, M. E. P., Steen, T. A., Park, N., & Peterson, C. (2005). Positive psychology progress: Empirical validation of interventions. *American Psychologist, 60*(5), 410–421. Retrieved from http://www.ppc.sas.upenn.edu/articleseligman.pdf.

[26] The VIA Character Web site has lots of resources on strengths. Use this link http://www.viacharacter.org/www/Research/Research-Findings#nav.

It is a subjective questionnaire based on your own perception of your strengths, so please understand it is not a "perfect" ranking. Even the lower ranked strengths can still be strengths. The purpose is to be able to recognize your strengths, which is vital information as you begin to build your brand and strategy. Most people are very aware of their weaknesses and flaws but not necessarily as aware of their strengths. Your top strengths are the basis of your signature brand, because they represent the things that come naturally to you.

It's common for people to take their top strengths for granted, but they highlight your unique contribution to society. The act of identifying and developing your signature strengths over just a two-week period can positively impact your happiness level and decrease depression symptoms.[27]
Upon completion of the questionnaire, ask yourself if you agree with the results, or do you think you have other strengths? Allow yourself to get curious with how your strengths show up in your life.

_____

_____

_____

_____

_____

_____

_____

_____

Select the five strengths that you think best describe you. They might be the strengths you use most often or the ones that make you feel the most energized and engaged.

1. _____

_____

_____

2. _____

_____

_____

3. _____

_____

_____

4. _____

_____

[27] Seligman, M. E. P., Steen, T. A., Park, N., & Peterson, C. (2005). Positive psychology progress: Empirical validation of interventions. *American Psychologist, 60*(5), 410–421.

5. _____

How can you use these strengths throughout the week to help you achieve your goals?

_____
_____
_____
_____
_____

Utilizing Your Strengths

Are there any challenges you are facing in your life right now that you might use your strengths to work through that obstacle?

(Note: Try to select a manageable problem and not something you would consider a lifetime concern. Think of which strengths you can use to move this issue forward in a positive direction. You might also find that your weaker strengths are the cause of the issue, or there might be certain strengths you want to call on more frequently to solve the problem. Explore your options. You might want to share your insights with a friend who could add perspective.)

If you get stuck, develop clarity on what outcome you would like to see. The following questions can help:

- What does the perfect solution look like?
- How have your strengths helped you achieve your goals?
- What other strengths can you use to achieve your goals?
- What have you tried in the past that might work in this situation?
- What if there were no challenges?
- Is there an alternative way to approach the situation using your strengths?

_____
_____
_____
_____
_____
_____
_____
_____

CHAPTER 4

The Power of Your Beliefs

I believe that women can be taught to use money as a *powerful* tool to live meaningful lives and to change the world. I also believe that female leaders must advocate and support all women in finance. I believe women with this power can create amazing results. *This is my "why."* It is the reason for this book and it is the belief that supports my values and my vision which I discuss in Chapter 10.

Kate reported to me when I worked as Vice President for Shared Services at Travelport, a spin-off from Cendant in Parsippany, NJ. She was an excellent employee and very bright. I was surprised that over the fifteen years that she had been with the company, she had never been promoted and still worked as a financial analyst. She was quiet, kept to herself, and seemed unsure of herself.

My department, shared services, was tasked to develop the capital budget for the entire company. The capital budget is the result of an evaluation of potentially large project investments such as building a new plant or investing in a long-term venture, and it has strategic consequences. When I asked Kate to present the capital budget to the president and the managing directors, she told me that she didn't understand it well enough.

She told me she was not good at speaking in front of people and she didn't feel capable of answering any questions. I told her that she was wrong and that she knew the budget and what she was doing better than anyone but she didn't believe me.

I leaned on Kate a lot. She helped me establish controls around the capital budgeting process and create a system to identify the top Net Present Value (NPV) projects to recommend to the president. It might not seem like a big deal but when I came to the business, each of the individual business unit managing directors had their own capital budgeting process and means of evaluating capital spending. Determination of how capital was spent at the

L. Mattia, *Gender on Wall Street*,
https://doi.org/10.1007/978-3-319-75550-2_4

company level was based on a less robust analysis and was all about making a "deal." I suppose this culture came from a history of private equity deals when the company was cobbled together by investment bankers. They bought and sold businesses to create value rather than executing on a strategic operational plan intended to increase economic value over the long term.

The reports that Kate helped create provided the company president with value-added analysis so he could make decisions based on what would increase the long-term bottom line and the ROI of the company. The president was thrilled. Although the wheeler-dealer managing director crew were not as thrilled, they were impressed. They knew this was the right way to run a business for the long term.

The turning point for Kate was when we began having monthly capital budgeting meetings to discuss the various projects and I made certain she attend. At first, management was resistant toward me bringing members of my team. When questions came up, I asked Kate to explain the analysis since she had prepared it and was the most knowledgeable of the detail. I assured her that I was there to answer any questions that she got stuck on but that I needed her to explain the specifics I was not involved in. It worked well because she answered most of the questions. I only interjected during the more heated discussions.

Initially, Kate was clearly uncomfortable but became more self-confident as she realized she had the answers. She was proud of her work and it showed. The management group was impressed and surprised that she was so capable and knowledgeable. Kate was surprised too. She had been operating under a belief system that did not support her. In fact, it held her back.

As the months went on, she started to believe in her ability to communicate and influence the decision-making process around the company's capital expenditures. She began to talk to upper management and even her peers.

It was amazing to watch her transformation, and it was rewarding for me since I knew I helped her. Once Kate began to believe in her value, her confidence and personal power blossomed. Her contribution to the business exploded. When our own beliefs hold us back, sometimes the only other remedy is for someone else to believe in us. I believed in Kate and that got the ball rolling; but in the end, she needed to rise up and believe in herself.

Finally, Kate was recognized in front of the group for her participation in a mission-critical and visible assignment. It was the catalyst for helping her change her beliefs about herself, which effected how other people saw her. Certainly, people at Travelport had a perception about Kate but her own opinions reinforced their perception and ultimately, it was her new opinions of herself that would change their perception.

We are more in control of how others see us than we realize or take responsibility for. To be considered a player and a candidate for promotion, Kate needed to first change her beliefs and then others followed. Months later, when a finance manager position opened up, I had no problem convincing the managing director of the business unit to hire her.

Mentor Insight: Make yourself visible and show the business what you can do. Ask your boss to help you identify opportunities to do that and make a strategic plan to showcase your strengths. Your boss will be happy to help since you have already built a relationship with him/her and your contributions are valued.

One day, after she became manager, Kate and I went out for lunch. She told me she was considering going back to school to become a Certified Financial Planner (CFP). Of course, I was very supportive as a big believer in education, continuous learning, and in obtaining certifications of competency. I also thought she would be a great financial planner.

Five years ago, Kate sat and passed her CFP® exam. She decided to start her own firm. Today, she is a member of the XY Network and is completely energized about her work. Of course, you need to believe in yourself and have confidence to start a business by yourself. She did it and I am so proud of her.

Conscious Engagement

There are numerous studies that show how limiting beliefs impact outcomes. For example, Vanessa Perry from George Washington University and Marlene Morris from the University of Southern California showed that people's ability to behave in their own best interest by saving, budgeting, and controlling spending is related to the person's self-perception of their ability to master those behaviors.[1] If someone believes they can do it, they pursue good behavior improving their well-being.

Dr. Perry and Dr. Morris's work supports other research showing an individual's self-beliefs influence their behavior which then becomes self-fulfilling. This work provides evidence that when individuals experience discrimination in employment, that person may become more and more sensitive to other negative events, which creates a downward spiral in denigrating confidence. If a woman experiences gender-related challenges as a result of unconscious bias or hostility, these experiences can reinforce negative beliefs about herself, and her beliefs begin to create a self-fulfilling reality. This is why you need to monitor and guard your beliefs to ensure harmful beliefs do not creep into your consciousness.

Kate would have been recognized a lot sooner if she held positive beliefs about her ability. Nobody knew her at Travelport—she was just *that woman* in the corner cubicle. Without strong beliefs in her ability, she had not developed her identity, tapped into her strengths, or created her brand to market to superiors and co-workers. They didn't know who she was or what

---

[1] Perry, V. G., & Morris, M. D. (2005). Who is in control? The role of self perception, knowledge, and income in explaining consumer financial behavior. *Journal of Consumer Affairs, 39*(2), 299–313.

she stood for. This is why creating positive beliefs and developing a personal brand is so important. It is the only way to claim your career.

I use the word "claim" because conscious engagement and empowerment isn't something someone gives you; it's something you take. You do so by metaphorically reaching out and seizing it. The dictionary defines the verb "to claim" as to take as the rightful owner, to assert in the face of possible contradiction. In contrast, "to receive" is to come into possession of: to act as receptacle or container for; to accept as authoritative or true.

You, and no one else, are (or should be) in charge of your financial career. It's critical to know what conscious engagement is and what is not. It's being responsible and accountable for your financial career and making certain it fits within your life purpose.

Claiming your financial career means resolving to control your destiny by making career decisions based upon what is best for you and your circumstances. This means being responsible and accountable to yourself without any excuses. By laying claim to your career, you'll be in a better position to develop resources to achieve your goals.

Some readers may not care all that much about their career. Maybe it's just not that important, or you've chosen to put your energy toward other life matters: your family, your faith, your friends, the planet, and people in need. Conscious engagement in your career could significantly help to actively support those life matters.

Perhaps you don't care about your career but you do care about gender equality; you want to be respected and elevate your social status. Maybe you don't like feeling dependent or vulnerable and want to be able to make your own choices. Conscious engagement in your career can help you achieve these goals too, which creates empowerment.

Conscious Engagement = Empowerment

- Education with a mastery of technical skills and awareness of challenges.
- Motivation inspired by your values.
- Protection against challenges.
- Ownership of your present and future.
- Winning beliefs in yourself.
- Engagement by successfully utilizing your strengths.
- Responsibility to yourself.

Responsibility to one's self is a new concept for many women. Women from prior generations were brought up to believe that their relationships and responsibilities to others are more important than being responsible to ourselves. We focus on everyone else's needs: partners, children, parents, or whomever. At times, we allow others to think, talk, and act on our behalf instead of solving our own problems or taking control of our own lives.

PERSONAL BELIEFS

Women also tend to hold certain beliefs about pursuing a career, many of them unconscious. These beliefs may have been instilled by family, friends, teachers, or simply by the culture. Step back from all of that for a minute and think about what *you truly believe*. Ripping away the veil of unconsciousness is a critical step to conscious engagement.

If you believe that money is the root of all evil, examine this belief. Is it blocking your prosperity, happiness, or general success? If you believe that a woman who pursues a career doesn't value her family, could this belief be blocking your motivation to do well at work or seek a promotion?

The vast majority of us never think about our beliefs at all. We just act on them and live by them and then are often bewildered or upset with the results. Our beliefs follow natural laws similar to kinetic or atomic energy, electricity, or any other form of natural force. Real consequences ensue from your beliefs and thoughts.

Let's say you believe that you don't deserve to have a successful career. That thought can prevent you from taking action to get it. Our thoughts lead to feelings, and our feelings lead to action (or inaction) that affects the circumstances in our lives. For example, if you see yourself as a victim of gender discrimination, you might become apathetic, which leads to lethargy. Hence, you won't take action and you'll miss out on opportunities.

It's important to understand the difference between feelings and thoughts. Career decisions should stem from our thoughts, not from our feeling, which is why we need to manage our beliefs. Beliefs about your career, your ability, and your potential could impede your progress.

Not only are certain beliefs limiting, but if you're unaware of them, they can trigger fears or cause resistance to positive work behavior. Observers either evaluate these behaviors as illogical (if they know someone is capable) or assume the person is not capable. Your beliefs are holding you back if you find yourself doing things that are self-defeating such as:

- Staying in a job you don't like.
- Putting off looking for the kind of job you want.
- Allowing yourself to be abused at work or working too many hours on activities you know will not help you to meet your work goals.
- Putting off the work required to get an extra certification or license that will lead to higher compensation or a promotion.

Understanding where your beliefs come from can help you decide if you value the belief. Is it helping you achieve your life purpose and your goals? If not, it is time to ditch those beliefs. They will only sabotage your progress and efforts.

Mentor Insight: You might be working against yourself. If you don't believe in yourself, who will? You need to make sure your unconscious beliefs are not sabotaging your confidence and your ability to communicate your brand.

I'll share a personal story about how unconscious beliefs are developed. It took me a long time to figure out why I felt the way I did about the business world and money in general, but after I discovered conscious engagement, I was able to examine my beliefs with greater clarity.

Growing up, my parents believed that money was evil. They thought people who worked for money were greedy. (No wonder they didn't have any money!) Yet, whenever she had a little extra, my mother gave her money away to the Endowment of the Arts and various other charities. When the time came for me to go to college, there was nothing put away to pay for it. I worked full time in high school and college to save up for my education.

Yes, it was character building (and I wouldn't be the person I am today) but it was hard to work forty hours a week in high school and college. There were many things I missed out on. When I graduated high school my father found a job after several years of unemployment. My parents moved to Massachusetts for the job, leaving me in New Jersey to find a place to live.

No, they did not pay my bills, or my health insurance, or my phone bill (this was in the dark ages before cell phones). They left me to figure it all out myself. My parents loved me very much and they were wonderful parents, but they were unable to help me financially since they were struggling themselves. They also had my younger brother to take care of.

Later, I learned how badly my mother felt about the situation and leaving me on my own at seventeen. None of it made sense. My parents seemed to value the things that money could buy (like an education for their daughter) but they did not value money as a necessary tool to buy that education. This is a perfect example of a belief that is inconsistent with values. Not only did their choices indicate a misunderstanding of money, they demonstrate how beliefs can sabotage your values.

TRADITIONAL SOCIAL PRESSURE

Diane and I were pregnant at the same time. We spent a lot of time commiserating about the difficulties of working with children and discussing what each of us would do after giving birth. I had already hired an au pair from Japan and knew I was planning to go back to work.

Diane, on the other hand, was struggling with what to do. Her husband and mother were pressuring her to stay home and be a "good" mother. I already knew that I would not be a "good" mother if I stayed home. I tried that with my first child years ago and quickly learned how miserable I was. Just to feel the sense of accomplishment I was addicted to, I washed the floor three times a day.

After we each had our children, I went back to work but Diane did not. I suspected that she wouldn't be satisfied staying at home. After all, she had a very successful career in finance and an MBA from Stanford. Several months after the kids were born, we got together for a dinner/play date at a local restaurant. Diane confided that she was losing it. She missed the intellectual stimulation of work.

To stay home with your children or go back to work is a common dilemma and very personal decision. I have the highest respect for women who are able to sacrifice their own needs for the good of the family. It is a noble mission. The problem, however, is when women feel compelled to make the decision to stay home because they were told by someone else that they should, or worse, they feel it is what society thinks they should do. This is when you have given up your own power to choose. Often women don't take the time to think about what they really need in connection with their values and strength, which is the opposite of being empowered. I equate empowerment with taking responsibility for myself first, not to the detriment of those around me, but to more effectively take responsibility for them as well.

If you believe a mother should be at home with her children, then *you* are making the choice: Great. However, people develop their careers over a span of forty to forty-five years. It is doubtful that your children will need you for all of those years as much as they need you during the first ten years or so. You might want to consider returning to your career at some point. One of the challenges of leaving the job market is that it's not always easy to reenter. Job prospects and income potential could be impacted.

Perhaps there are other options to also consider. Financial firms are finally beginning to understand they need to become more compliant if they want to attract and retain top female talent. Financial services can be very flexible if you are working at the right firm and if you are in the right job. I know many women and men who work from home and their clients have no idea where they are; they just know that they are being served. As long as you can perform your job, there are some firms that do not issue a penalty for a modified work environment. Being able to articulate what you want is the first step to getting what you need to be happy with your work environment. Many firms are willing to go out of their way to accommodate.

Some women choose to stay home after a baby because they are frustrated with their career, and they don't know how to create a strategy to succeed. This is a particularly disturbing scenario because they are not making the choice to be with their family; they are making the choice to run away from an unrewarding work experience. Most women will not admit to this thinking, and perhaps it is unconscious, but it's not in the woman's best interest.

A recent Australian research study showed that women leave senior roles in finance due to a combination of work frustration and the availability of other options outside the job. Interestingly, the women's responses did not indicate the reason for leaving was due to family responsibilities. Instead, the women indicated they left due to cultural issues related to an arrogant, competitive, environment with a lack of flexible opportunities allowing for work–life balance, and management support for women.[2] This study implies some women may choose to leave their career due to dissatisfaction rather than values.

Another study looked into the Chartered Financial Analyst (CFA®) profession specifically. It provides insight on what motivates female CFA® members and how they become frustrated. The study compared three specific values—tradition, conformity, and achievement—of CFA® members to the values of the general population. The researcher focused on tradition and conformity as proxies for whether the participant held traditional gender roles. The third value, achievement, served as an opposing force to traditional gender roles.

In other words, if a woman holds achievement as a top value, she is not as prone to accepting the limitations that come with the gender social construct. This is exactly what they found: Women who choose finance are less prone to conform to social gender norms and are more interested in achievement than women who do not pursue finance. Even more interesting, female CFA®s are more achievement oriented than male CFA®s. Female CFA®s are high achievers and were most likely taught that they could do whatever they aspired toward.[3] They believe they will achieve success. They are not susceptible to social sabotage or societal "norms" that dictate how they should lead their lives.

Self-Sabotage

Leanne worked for me as a paraplanner when I first left the corporate world. She had all the makings to be successful in the finance industry. She was smart, personable, and eager to learn.

Since she was brand new to finance, I expected her to make some mistakes, as everyone does. Instead of working through those mistakes or asking for help, she tried to cover them up by making excuses or even avoiding the necessary action to fix it. She spent a lot of time talking to other people in the office and the customers, who all adored her.

I tried to schedule meetings to help her but something always came up. She was constantly apologizing for taking up my time, and then apologizing for apologizing. If I needed her to correct something, she got red in the face and said she was incompetent. At the end of the day, her work was never complete. She bemoaned her intention to do better tomorrow.

Ultimately, she admitted that she was a procrastinator, but unfortunately she failed to recognize that she was the only person who could change that. I

[2] Neck, C. (2015). Disappearing women: Why do women leave senior roles in finance? Further evidence. *Australian Journal of Management, 40*(3), 511–537.

[3] Adams, Barber, Odean. (2016). Family, Values and Women in Finance.

tried to coach her but she decided she didn't like the pressure of office work and took a job managing a retail shop instead.

Mentor Insight: Know that you are not alone. Everyone has moments when they don't operate in their own best interest. We all shoot ourselves in the foot and make things harder for ourselves from time to time. This only becomes a problem when we repeat specific behaviors or embrace beliefs that get in the way of our success.

Procrastination and self-effacing behavior are two of the more common ways women hold themselves back. The most effective way to change this behavior is to recognize it and make a firm commitment to change. Then, be patient with yourself and continue to work on it. Change doesn't ever happen instantly but taking personal responsibility does wonders toward making it happen. Break it in steps, look for small changes and celebrate them.

Mentor Insight: Please do not beat yourself up for past behavior. You're only able to change if you relinquish judgment and denounce past behavior as something that you refuse to own or associate with. You must be patient and compassionate with yourself if old patterns resurface. In later chapters, we'll discuss how you can redirect your behavior in a productive fashion to achieve your goals. For now, just be aware of what isn't working and take the time to examine core beliefs that may be sabotaging your behavior.

EXERCISE: EXAMINING YOUR BELIEFS

Take the following quiz to determine which beliefs about your abilities might be preventing you from reaching your goals. Keep in mind that some beliefs may be unconscious, so you might need to think hard to see whether they apply to you. Circle the beliefs that resonate with you.

1. The love of money is the root of all evil.
2. I don't deserve to earn a lot of money.
3. He/She doesn't deserve to earn lot of money.
4. There is not enough money to go around.
5. If I earn a little more than I need, someone else has to go without enough.
6. If I am successful, people will hate me.
7. I am not good in math so I shouldn't even try to understand finance.
8. If I have a career, then I won't have enough time for my family.
9. If I am miserable at work, my family will know they are more important to me.
10. If I make a lot of money, I will be betraying my father, who never made much money.
11. If I make a lot of money, I will be betraying my husband (or significant other), who is not able to make as much money.
12. I am not that smart, so I should not be successful.
13. I am not as smart as the men so I cannot expect to receive the same pay or opportunities.
14. If I assert myself, I will upset other person and ruin our relationship.
15. Money is hard to deal with.
16. Money is hard to get.
17. You have to do unethical things to make a lot of money.
18. To save money, you have to do without things.
19. If I ask for what I need, people will see me as selfish.
20. I can't have a career and family life.
21. Pursuit of a financial career is not spiritual.
22. You have to do lots of things you don't like in order to get money.
23. I do not have enough to share or give away.
24. Accepting money obligates me.
25. It's better to take less than my due to avoid sticky situations.
26. To be a valuable person, I have to work more for less money than other people do.
27. Having money stops you from being happy.
28. Money spoils you.
29. I will never be good enough.
30. If I don't feel bad about past investment mistakes, I will make the same mistakes again.
31. If I don't worry about my financial future, I will be broke.
32. Men are inherently better at math than women.
33. Being highly conscious about every single penny is the best course.

34. Never buy anything that you don't need.
35. If I were a smart woman, I could easily support myself.
36. If I was a good looking woman, I could have married someone with money.
37. I always rent because owning a house would be too scary.
38. I can attribute my success to luck.
39. Working mothers are selfish.
40. Worrying about money is tacky.
41. If I make a million dollars, I might lose it. Then I would feel stupid and hate myself.
42. I want to have a lot of money when I get old. Then people will be nice to me.
43. I never want people to know I have a lot of money because people are mean to rich people.
44. If I get paid for my work, then people will discover that I'm a fraud.
45. My father/mother will like me better if I spend conservatively.
46. Women are not as savvy with money as men.
47. Women are not as confident as men with investments.
48. If I spend money on something that breaks, I'm stupid.
49. If I am lucky, management will promote me.
50. Men have better leadership and management skills than women.
51. Other _____

Pick the top two beliefs that you suspect could be sabotaging your success. When reviewing each belief ask yourself these six questions:

Sabotaging Belief 1 _____

_____
_____

1. Where did this belief come from?

_____
_____
_____
_____
_____

2. Why do I believe this?

_____
_____
_____
_____
_____

3. How does this belief prevent me from achieving my goals?

_____
_____
_____
_____
_____

4. What is the probability that this belief is realistic or plausible?

_____
_____
_____
_____
_____

5. What if I changed this belief? How could that alter the achievement of my goals?

_____
_____
_____
_____

6. How can I reframe this belief to diffuse its power?

Sabotaging Belief 2 _____

1. Where did this belief come from?

2. Why do I believe this?

3. How does this belief prevent me from achieving my goals?

4. What is the probability that this belief realistic or plausible?

5. What if I changed this belief? How could that alter the achievement of my goals?

_____
_____
_____
_____
_____

6. How can I reframe this belief to diffuse its power?

_____
_____
_____
_____
_____

CHAPTER 5

The Magic of Self-Confidence

Ginny, the mother of one of my daughter's friends—whom I am also friendly with—approached me a few years ago to talk about my career. She was fascinated that I was working at the university, still working with a fee-only practice, and involved in several other side projects.

Ginny had lived in England for a time, due to her husband's job. She spoke about her "fortuitous" career back in England as a manager for a hedge fund. She told me how a friend of the family had hired her to work for him and how "The fund did very well because he had all the tools and research staff to help me make good calls to execute the strategy." Not once did she say anything about her critical thinking abilities, decision-making skills, or technical competence that contributed to the effective execution of the hedge fund strategy.

Now back in New Jersey, she had not been able to find satisfactory work. Her husband was the general manager of a major corporation and travelled a lot, and Ginny felt relegated to taking care of the home and children. She also felt like she didn't have any value in the financial world and that her previous experience had been due to a lucky break.

As I listened, I recognized that Ginny seemed unable to acknowledge her own abilities and contribution to the success of the firm—a necessary component for a strong self-image. This low self-image must have made it easy for her to decide she could not find a comparable job, and that it was probably a good time to become a stay at home mother. The problem with this decision was that she wasn't happy—it was inconsistent with her values and vision.

She went on to explain that she didn't think she was smart enough to manage a hedge fund or any investment fund. Her experience in England had been a fluke where she was supported by a great staff of people. She sounded like she bought into the myth that women are not suited for logical or analytical thought. She seemed oblivious to her own expertise and competence,

© The Author(s) 2018
L. Mattia, *Gender on Wall Street*,
https://doi.org/10.1007/978-3-319-75550-2_5

and like many women, had allowed her power to remain latent due to a lack of confidence.

Initially, the conversation started out with her inquiring how I could possibly work full time, own a wealth management firm, and teach at a university. She also wanted to know how I had the time to be active in my church and the local soup kitchen. What about my children?

I heard three messages through her questions. The first was one of judgment; she was critical of my hubris to think that my behavior was appropriate. Women are supposed to be dependent, domestic, and certainly not ambitious. The second message was one of admiration. But it was the third message around empowerment that I wanted to address, her own yearning for a meaningful career.

I explained to her that I was highly motivated toward achievement. My lifetime goal was to positively transform lives. It still is uncommon to hear women discuss a desire for power of any kind but I could tell that it resonated. She wanted to feel a sense of achievement too.

As we talked, she asked about my four children. The two boys are already out of college and making their own mark on the world. The two girls were young at the time—in 5th and 7th grades—and developing their own confidence and abilities and ultimately their personal power. I explained to Ginny that my children are my number one priority and that, like her, I was brought up with a high level of responsibility. This level of responsibility drives my motivation for power and how I influence other people's lives.

My girls see my behavior and what I am trying to achieve and they help me. They help me prepare my lesson plans for the university by avoiding television and sitting with me in the living room while we read. They also help with a lot of chores that most children don't do but they know their mom needs the support. I don't consider this a bad thing or feel like I'm not being responsible. I think one of the greatest responsibilities I have is to show them how to reach their potential.

Both girls assume they are also going to be leaders in their chosen profession, when the time comes. I have told them it is much easier to do that before they find a husband, get married, and have children. I tell them that they should have the full confidence and personal power to determine the direction of their lives. I hope they are empowered to reject external forces that attempt to control their resources.

What I have been trying to teach my girls reflects the idea of obtaining legitimate power, which will enable them to be more open about their demands and needs. In retrospect, my rationale reflects a responsibility orientation which many psychologists attribute toward decision making and self-efficacy or confidence.

Ginny seemed to be inspired by our conversation. She understood that we were talking about confidence, personal empowerment for ourselves, and also for our girls. Power is not about being a winner or loser; it's about the freedom to develop our own abilities.

I spoke to Ginny again recently. She told me she had inquired about pursuing a second masters in finance, which will help her achieve her career aspirations. She lamented that her girls did not have enough positive images of women. They continue to see stereotypes of women in the media and in the community, and she wants to change that. She also agreed that we, as mothers, need to be strong role models for our girls and project confidence, personal responsibility, and power so that we can break the vicious cycle of female disempowerment.

Mentor Insight: Your beliefs are the internal building blocks that help you develop your personal power and confidence. They are the single biggest influence on your self-confidence, which is critical for taking personal responsibility for the direction of your own career. Beware the "woe is me; I'm not good enough" path. It's a sure fire way to remain standing still.

CONFIDENCE RESEARCH

Research indicates that women, in general, are less confident than men, even women in the financial industry. Researchers have identified gender differences in confidence between college-age males and females, and male and female financial experts.[1] Confidence can be described as a self-awareness of one's knowledge and is usually linked to education and experience. It is directly related to one's beliefs about their abilities.

In past studies, researchers have controlled for many differences that could explain why women are less confident. Factors such as age, business experience, level of education, credit hours in accounting and finance, or work history could all be indicators of why women working in finance and investing are less confident than men.

Using survey data from 2047 German households, Christina Bannier and Milena Schwarz (née Neubert) from University of Giessen in Germany found that highly educated women undermine their own ability to accumulate wealth if they are under-confident.[2] Lack of confidence may be rational when knowledge or capability is inadequate but it is puzzling when a woman has adequate knowledge. The findings indicate that women need to align their confidence with their abilities.

---

[1] Garrison, S., & Gutter, M. (2010). 2010 outstanding AFCPE@ conference paper: Gender differences in financial socializaion and willingness to take financial risks; Chen, H., & Volpe, R. P. (2002). Gender differences in personal financial literacy among college students. *Financial Services Review, 11*(3), 289; Webster, R. L., & Ellis, T. S. (1996). Men's and women's self-confidence in performing financial analysis. *Psyhological Reports, 79*(Suppl. 3), 1251–1254.

[2] Bannier, C. E., & Neubert, M. (2016). Gender differences in financial risk-taking: The role of financial literacy and risk tolerance. *Economics Letters, 145*, 130–135.

As a finance professor, I have argued that we must focus on influencing women's self-beliefs when teaching technical financial skills. I was brought in as a visiting professor at Texas Tech University to create a special topics program for this primary purpose specifically targeted toward the women in the financial planning degree program. The workshop included exercises from this book and introduced students to the idea of networking with other women by creating an advocacy circle, which we will discuss in Chapter 12, as part of their personal strategy.

Just as one's beliefs impact one's confidence, so do emotions. Researchers have started to recognize how negative emotions, such as stress and worry, can diminish confidence, which results in a reduced commitment toward pursuing goals. Researchers have found that financial stress caused by a decline in income, personal bankruptcy, or investment losses provoke negative financial decisions, decrease self-confidence, and impact the ability to work with money.[3] Stress caused by other factors such as workplace bullying also creates social stress and impacts the ability to perform at work.[4]

Female financial advisors who are personally stressed due to a hostile work environment, unequal pay, or isolation (to be discussed in Part II of this book) experience a direct affront to their confidence. Financial advisors rely on their emotional state to judge their own abilities. Therefore, anxiety and/ or feelings of helplessness are unhealthy conditions that impair cognitive processes and obstruct job performance.

But do not despair, there are ways to overcome work-place challenges. A recent British study explored the use of personal strengths at work in a financial services firm.[5] Through structured interviews, participants described the value they derived from using their strengths, which led to what the authors identified as a "virtuous circle." A virtuous circle is a chain of events that reinforce themselves through a feedback loop with positive results. The more positive the participant's experience, the higher their confidence.

* Mentor Insight: Your personal strengths identified in the Chapter 3 exercise can be used to significantly increase your confidence. Focus on how you can use those strengths to achieve your goals.

[3]Grable, J. E., & Joo, S.-H. (2001). A subsequent study of the relationships between self-worth and financial beliefs, behavior, and satisfaction. *Journal of Family and Consumer Sciences, 93*(5), 25; Kim, J., & Garman, E. T. (2004). Financial stress, pay satisfaction, and workplace performance. *Compensation & Benefits Review, 36*(1), 69–76; Joo, S.-H., & Grable, J. E. (2000). Improving employee productivity: The role of financial counseling and education. *Journal of Employment Counseling, 37*(1), 2–15.

[4]Vartia, M. A. (2001). Consequences of workplace bullying with respect to the well-being of its targets and the observers of bullying. *Scandinavian Journal of Work, Environment & Health,* 63–69; Bond, S. A., Tuckey, M. R., & Dollard, M. F. (2010). Psychosocial safety climate, workplace bullying, and symptoms of posttraumatic stress. *Organization Development Journal, 28*(1), 37.

[5]Elston & Bonniwel. (2011). A grounded theory study of the value derived by women in the financial services of a coaching intervention to help them identify their strengths and practice using them in the workplace.

The British study provides evidence that increased confidence can reduce the frequency and impact of hidden challenges that many women experience in financial services firms. By focusing on how they could be successful in their jobs and building up their confidence, the participants also positively affected how they felt about their jobs, their relationships at work, their commitment which increased their overall engagement, and even their fit, within the financial organization.

Being Authentic

What does confidence in female financial advisors look like? Effectively managing confidence and personal power in business relationships sometimes requires encouragement.

I mentored Mary, a CFP® a few years ago. She had a great deal of confidence but she wasn't sure how to influence her partners to achieve an equitable agreement. Partnerships are interesting relationships. Often times, they can be like a marriage but each partner tends to be a lot more selfish due to a lack of emotional commitment.

Mary was the key partner in her firm. She had superior credentials and experience compared to most advisors in the industry, including her partners. Although her contribution to the business was substantial, she felt like she was not heard, and described her status as "second class" next to the men.

At one of our sessions, she described a confrontational conversation with Carl, the founding partner of her firm. After months of attempting to gain agreement on the adaption of a benefit policy to include health insurance, she was annoyed at the lip service and lack of progress. The insurance was part of their initial partnership agreement but it seemed Carl was attempting to renege.

I suggested that Mary was not using her personal power in a constructive manner. I advised her to exercise her confidence in a way that satisfied her needs as well as the needs of the business partnership. Hinting at the issue and complaining was not an effective way to reach a concrete resolution. I suggested to Mary that Carl might even resent her because her indirect attempt to influence the outcome could be interpreted as manipulative. Either way, it was not working.

Mary admitted there were several things that had been bothering her and she wasn't sure how to deal with them. When she joined the partnership five years prior, she took a significant pay cut with the thought that if she grew the business, her compensation would increase.

Although there had been a minor increase to her compensation, it was not as lucrative as she expected. Carl had decided to increase fixed costs to absorb future growth. She was frustrated that he had unilaterally decided to do this without recognizing her sacrifice and her compensation expectations. She thought the least the firm could do was honor the initial agreement that included benefits once the firm reached $150M in AUM. They had been talking about this for eight months with no conclusion in sight.

By not tapping into her confidence, Mary did not assert herself. I suggested she take a more direct approach. I asked Mary why she did not try to have a candid conversation with Carl. Additionally, I suggested she change the focus of her argument to a desire to help the firm and emphasize how her contribution would allow the firm to grow.

Mary went back to Carl, recited her commitment and what she had done for the firm. She then affirmed her continued commitment and said, "I know you value my work and therefore will understand that providing the health benefits we agreed upon will allow me to continue to contribute. If that is not the case, then I need to make other arrangements." From Carl's perspective, his dominant role was derived from his rank and position as founder of the firm. I suspect that he expected Mary to defer her personal power as someone with a lower status, both as a non-founder and as a woman.

Mary later recounted what happened as a result of her direct and assertive approach. She had exercised her legitimate (as the primary rain maker in the business) and expert (as a highly educated and credentialed partner) power. She said it was clear Carl was not used to assertive and direct discussion. He viewed the discussion as confrontational. He was accustomed to being in power hierarchically and physically (he was very tall and physically intimidating). He did not react well to Mary's direct approach. He turned very red and did not say much during their initial meeting.

At a follow-up meeting Carl requested several days later, he asked Mary why she was so demanding and he appeared angry. Mary simply told him that she was advocating for herself. In the end, the partners agreed to provide the health insurance promised and Carl agreed to restrain the firm's fixed costs in the future.

Mary felt validated that she had expressed her dissatisfaction with how she was treated in the firm. However, she was aware that the only way she would get Carl to respect and comply with her needs was to revert to a winner-loser power model using threats. For the time being, this was not insurmountable even though she preferred a more collaborative approach to working with her partner.

Mentor Insight: Develop your confidence and exercise your personal power with the understanding that you will only get as much nonsense as you are willing to put up with. Know your worth so that you can find satisfying career arrangements.

Sometime later, Mary completed the exercise at the end of Chapter 2: Analyzing Your Career Values. She realized her values were not being met through the partnership and she did not want to remain in this type of power struggle. She asked Carl to buy her out. She was confident in her marketability and what she had to offer other firms.

As expected, Carl did not handle her request well and turned it into a legal battle. Eventually, he lost the case. In spite of the unpleasantness, Mary planned her exit in way that would smooth the transition in a constructive fashion and have as little impact on the clients as possible. Just months after leaving the firm, she received numerous offers from other firms asking her to join them. Mary's belief in her own self-worth, her confidence, and her personal power enabled her to find a much more suitable firm.

Mentor Insight: Don't let a stressful environment destroy your confidence. Either employ conscious engagement strategies to alleviate stress or find a less stressful environment. Stress and anxiety are poison to your self-efficacy.

Using tools from positive psychology, discussed in the Chapter 3 exercise, we can train our minds to focus on what is working in our career and avoid what is not. Positive psychology is about focusing on the development of skills that help us to handle the stressful work environments that many women inevitably deal with. It teaches us how to create more positive settings in which we can succeed instead of struggle.

The intention is to decrease the frequency of negative emotions while increasing the frequency of positive ones. One great way to do this is to spend time celebrating our wins and focusing on the times when we are at our best. Understanding and using our natural strengths throughout the workday delivers positive results and can ultimately lead toward improved overall well-being in the financial services career of your choosing.

Exercise: Developing Your Confidence

This is a powerful visualization and journaling exercise. I have walked many women's groups through this process with great success. This exercise requires you to reflect on a time in your life when you were proud of your performance. This gives you an opportunity to identify your personal strengths and passions. It is intended to create an awareness of what you like about yourself. Many women who have participated in this exercise have told me that they learned something about themselves that they were not consciously aware of.

1. Before you start writing, the idea is to spend time visualizing the situation. Find a relaxing place to sit comfortably and quietly, for this ten-minute visualization. Sitting quietly, allowing your thoughts to flow freely is a great way to become aware of your unconscious thoughts and to focus on what is most important to you.
2. Once you are comfortable, close your eyes and turn your attention to your breath. Simply focus your attention on your breath as it comes in; follow it through your nose all the way down to your lungs. Don't worry that you're not doing it right, just relax into your breath. Remain focused on your breath for several minutes. This is a form of meditation which relaxes and brings awareness to your mind.
3. As you breathe in and out, guide your thoughts to a recent time when you were proud of your performance. Imagine the place, the people you were with, smells, colors, almost as if you are watching a video. See yourself in that moment in time.

   - Who is with you?
   - Where are you?
   - What are your surroundings like?
   - What are you doing?
   - How are you behaving?
   - How do you feel about yourself?
   - How are other people behaving toward you?
   - How do you feel about them?

4. Once you open your eyes, spend another five minutes writing about this experience. Think of as many details about this moment in time as you can.

   - Why is this experience meaningful to you?
   - What personal qualities and strengths did you rely on?
   - How can you use these qualities and strengths in other work-related situations to achieve your goals?

The last part of this exercise can be powerful. Find someone who cares about you to share your experience with. Ask them what they think about your actions. Ask if they have feedback on why they think you were successful. Listen to their feedback and write it down. Their assessment will come in handy as you build your brand. Share your experience with as many people as you would like. People who care about you will enjoy learning more about this intimate part of you and your confidence will soar by remembering and focusing on your positive experience.

_____
_____
_____
_____
_____
_____
_____
_____
_____
_____
_____
_____
_____
_____
_____
_____
_____
_____
_____
_____
_____
_____
_____
_____
_____

PART II

The Gender-Specific Challenges

CHAPTER 6

The Prevalence of Unconscious Bias

Toni is a fund-raiser at a not-for-profit organization. She recently invited me to speak at a luncheon on the topic of Women and Philanthropy. During the Q&A, I had an opportunity to share some of the research about women and money. She came up to me after my talk and said that she was exactly the woman I had been speaking about. She had been a finance major. Working with numbers, money, and analysis was her passion. She wanted to work on Wall Street since she was thirteen. Her dream was answered when she got an internship in her senior year of college to work at Goldman Sachs.

The internship went well, and after she graduated, they offered her a full-time position. Toni quickly noticed how few women were in partner or managing director roles. Although there were plenty of women in the lower ranks, she didn't see women being promoted. It seemed like it was going to be a long struggle to be successful at the firm, especially because it appeared that the men were more supportive of the men. There seemed to be an unconscious bias against women in management.

Recently, Toni received an opportunity to go into fund-raising for the not-for-profit organization. Sufficiently frustrated with her future prospects at Goldman, she decided to make the change. Although she was happy in her current role, she laments that she was not successful at a traditional career in finance. I gave her my business card and told her to call me saying, "You would be a natural financial planner. You just need to find the right place and to develop a strategy on how to navigate your career." I have not heard back from her but I hope she becomes inspired to pursue her dream.

Mentor Insight: If you really want to succeed in financial services, do not let unconscious bias deter you. Instead, focus on your strategy, your technical skills, your Advocacy Circle, and your relationships. Unconscious bias is common but it has nothing to do with you personally. Don't let it scare you away from your passion.

© The Author(s) 2018
L. Mattia, *Gender on Wall Street*,
https://doi.org/10.1007/978-3-319-75550-2_6

Social and Gender Norms

Let me tell you a puzzling story. A young man named Jake came to my office to discuss his investments. He told me that his father died at the age of 55, when he was 20. Now 35 years later, he just celebrated his 55th birthday. He said. "I want to retire before it is too late and I need someone to take over my $4M investment portfolio. A family member, a Wall Street executive, has advised me on my investments for the past 35 years, but refuses to take over the management of my portfolio." I asked Jake if I could call the advisor to ask why. The Wall Street executive told me, "It is firm's policy. I cannot manage the portfolio because Jake is my son." How could that be?

I have told this anecdote many times at events centered on the topic of women and money, and I always get similar answers. Most people have to stop and think hard. Many ask if the advisor is the stepfather, if the parents were gay, if it was an older brother, or even if the father was a priest so his real "dad" was still alive. Of course, the advisor is Jake's mother.

I shared this narrative with a group of young ladies at a Women's Advocacy Retreat, which prepares women to develop strategies to be successful female financial planners. Even given the context of the group, the women struggled with the riddle. At this last retreat, there was a woman who was getting her masters in financial planning. She already had an undergraduate degree in sex and gender studies. Much to her surprise (and mine), she couldn't solve the puzzle.

Society has programmed us to think that Wall Street executives and financial professionals—people who truly understand money and investing—are men. The problem with this mind-set is that it logically means that women in finance are not the norm and that they are second choice. Further, this leads to an assumption that women working in a finance capacity aren't as competent. The danger of this old and outdated social construct is that it reinforces stereotypes, yet we aren't even aware of it. Hence, it is an unconscious bias—not malicious in intent but damaging just the same.

Unconscious bias is when discrimination and incorrect judgments occur due to stereotyping. It often occurs automatically without awareness. This bias is usually so ingrained in society that is goes unnoticed by most people.

Unconscious bias explains a lot about women's status in the financial world. Many firms have tried to reduce bias through education and increased awareness. However, a featured article in the March 2016 *Governance Directions* highlights the fact that organizations focused on unconscious bias training have ironically increased unconscious bias, creating more stereotyping, not less.[1] If you think about it, bias is not an error in judgment that can be corrected through a training regime since unconscious bias is exactly that—unconscious.

---

[1] Robertson, G., & Byrne, M. (2016). Getting gender balance "unstuck": Taking action with a new strategic approach. *Governance Directions, 68*(2), 79.

Of course, we all know that females are not inherently or biologically infe-rior in financial capability than males, and of course females deserve the same opportunities and the same level of potential earnings as a man who does the same job. But how can that happen if we all (males and females) have trouble answering a riddle that acknowledges a universally understood inequality? We have a problem that cannot be fixed overnight. Our social and gender norms have developed over many years, and it will take many years for the hidden biases to turn around. Even professionals who are well aware of their behavio-ral biases are still subject to them.

Although past female progress in financial services has been slow and appears to predict women will not achieve critical mass until the middle of the century, there is reason to believe that a bias shift could occur more quickly if assisted. As economist Jessica Pan at the National University of Singapore has demon-strated, occupational change is nonlinear and there are tipping patterns that can help expedite paradigm changes.[2] Looking at occupational shifts from 1940 through to 1990, her research showed that when more women move into his-torically all-male occupations, there are tipping patterns that affect occupational change. She identifies the tipping point ranging from 25 to 45%.

Pan's research is consistent with research related to the influence women have on boards. Research has shown that women influence the operation and financial performance of firms when at least 30% of the board directors are women. Since the average size board consists of ten members, three directors must be female.[3] In Pan's study, the female directors' influence was measured in terms of higher returns on equity (ROE) and earnings per share (EPS) than companies with no female directors. In a Catalyst study, the report found higher performance for companies with women board directors when comparing return on equity (ROE), return on sales (ROS), and return on invested capital (ROIC). Companies with a high representation of women board directors out-performed companies with low representation in these measures by 53%, 42%, and 66%, respectively.[4] This research is consistent with other studies which spec-ulate that as female representation increases in the financial professional work-force, women will become the norm, and the consequences associated with being "not the norm," "second choice," or "not as competent" will subside.

As women in finance, we can expedite this change through conscious engagement and helping women strategically prepare for financial careers. By encouraging women to enter into the financial services industry, supporting them to achieve success and empowering them to remain in the industry, we can reach the tipping point faster.

[2] Pan, J. (2015). Gender segregation in occupations: The role of tipping and social interac-tions. *Journal of Labor Economics, 33*(2), 365–408.

[3] Joy, L., Carter, N. M., Wagner, H. M., & Narayanan, S. (2007). The bottom line: Corporate performance and women's representation on boards. *Catalyst, 3*, 619–625.

[4] http://www.catalyst.org/media/companies-more-women-board-directors-experience-higher-financial-performance-according-latest.

Industry Efforts Are Slow

A recent survey of female millennials done by PricewaterhouseCoopers (PwC) found 60% of the women working in financial services said their employer was not doing enough to encourage diversity and 50% said promotions were biased toward men.[5] The study also surveyed leadership of 410 financial services firms, where the majority of the firms indicated they had a strategy to promote diversity. Clearly, there is a disconnect. Although the industry is beginning to become actively engaged in supporting women, progress is slow since culture is hard to change.

Dominique Beck and Ed Davis at Macquarie University in Sydney, Australia, reported a case study that investigated the experiences of senior women managers at Westpac, a financial firm. The firm was selected due to its reputation of promoting women, but the study showed how difficult it is to reverse unconscious bias in a culture developed over many years.[6]

At Westpac Banking Corporation, more commonly known as Westpac, a male gendered culture had been part of the organization since the firm was founded in 1817. Westpac is the second largest bank in Australia and New Zealand, with over 13 million customers and 1429 branches as of 2015.[7] Its name is a portmanteau of "Western-Pacific," and it is a multi-conglomerate firm with a commercial bank arm, a business bank that works with small to medium-size businesses (specializing in asset and equipment manufacturing), a wealth management arm called BT Financial Group (BTFG), and a 31% interest in an investment management group called BT Investment Management (BTIM).

The bank has committed to increase the number of female managers but progress has been slow and more difficult than management anticipated. Despite equal opportunity policies, gender inequality persisted as it is embedded in the organization's culture.[8]

Westpac was selected for the study because it is known as one of the most progressive and forward-thinking Australian corporations with decades of strategic focus on increasing gender diversity. Recognizing the need to change the culture, the company has reinforced flexible work practices including job sharing, grandparent leave, and flexibility for child and elder care. They have also promoted inspirational role models to drive the cultural shift. The company openly stated their targets, held management accountable to specific targets, and have created transparent gender policies and programs.

---

[5] PwC Female millennials in financial services.

[6] Beck, D., & Davis, E. (2005). EEO in senior management: Women executives in Westpac. *Asia Pacific Journal of Human Resources, 43*(2), 273–288.

[7] https://www.westpac.com.au/about-westpac/westpac-group/company-overview/our-businesses/.

[8] Beck, D., & Davis, E. (2005). EEO in senior management: Women executives in Westpac. *Asia Pacific Journal of Human Resources, 43*(2), 273–288.

Westpac was even the first private sector company to pay retirement benefits during unpaid parental leave, which can make a significant difference in closing the retirement savings gap that many women experience.[9] The company has created a quarterly "Women in Management" report and an annual "Workforce Indicators" report over the years to track progress and highlight diversity accomplishments and challenges.[10]

Despite these efforts and some progress toward achieving their goals, the case study highlights interviews from senior women at Westpac who recount experiences that underscore the same hidden challenges to advancement discussed in this book. The study demonstrates that equal employment and human resources policies are limited in their ability to ensure women are successful due to the inertia of unconscious bias.

One report related to the women at Westpac cited that strong-willed women at the leadership level were perceived as "dominatrix, a wicked witch, or a Rottwiler with lipstick."[11] These types of comments do not build confidence or encourage engagement. Coworkers viewed women who exhibited aggressive and competitive behaviors negatively. Several women expressed the difficulty in behaving businesslike and were perceived as aggressive.[12]

Although less blatant than in the past, cultural barriers and gender stereotypes still exist. Overall, efforts at both Westpac and other financial firms who are committed to female advancement have not yet achieved gender equity.

BEHAVIORAL BIAS

Financial professionals are trained in behavioral finance theory and the shortcuts that people use to make financial decisions. Behavioral finance theory attempts to reconcile behavioral departures from rationality by applying psychological principles to the financial decision-making process.[13] The theory and evidence were developed because scientists were unable to explain why people don't make rational financial and investment decisions and instead often behave in ways that are clearly in conflict with their own best interest. Scientists began to look for explanations from other cross-disciplinary fields such as psychology and found individuals have bounded rationality. They observed that people's decision making is limited due to lack of knowledge, uncertainty, and/or an overall

---

[9] https://www.wgea.gov.au/gender-equality-initiatives/westpac-banks-female-talent.

[10] Gillespie, J. (1999). Profiting from diversity: The Westpac experience. In G. O'Neill & R. Kramar (Eds.), *Australian human resources management: Current trends in management practice* (pp. 207–216). Warriewood, NSW: Business and Professional Publishing.

[11] Beck, D., & Davis, E. (2005). EEO in senior management: Women executives in Westpac. *Asia Pacific Journal of Human Resources, 43*(2), 273–288.

[12] Beck, D., & Davis, E. (2005). EEO in senior management: Women executives in Westpac. *Asia Pacific Journal of Human Resources, 43*(2), 273–288.

[13] Shefrin, H. (2010). Behavioralizing finance. *Foundations and Trends® in Finance, 4*(1–2), 1–184.

inability to prioritize and select optimum solutions. Initially, behavioral finance theory focused on cognitive heuristics related to financial decision making.

A wide range of financial decisions by corporations, investors, and even fiduciaries can be explained by behavioral theory. The behavioral tendency to allow social norms, desires, and beliefs to manipulate decision making has been seen in study after study. In fact, when individuals believe their decisions will be scrutinized by others, they are even further swayed to stick to social norms because they are easier to justify than going against the grain.

Many non-financial decisions are the result of using mental shortcuts, the path of least resistance, which explains why it can be easier to select a man instead of a woman for an important financial position. Time is precious and we all have many things tugging at us. This is exactly what creates behavioral/unconscious bias. We use past data, classifications, social norms, and other shortcuts to facilitate decision making.

Sex Typing

Close your eyes and think of an inspiring business leader you know personally or have read about. What is it about them that resonates for you? Is the person forceful, strong, dominant, competent, or possibly even a hero? Is the leader a woman? Chances are the answer to this last question is a disappointing "no."

Virginia Schein from Gettysburg College has researched women's progress in management and organizational behavior since the 1970s. She identified managerial sex typing as a major psychological barrier to the advancement of women. She compares her initial study to many other studies in countries such as Great Britain and Germany. The studies use the same measurement instruments and similar procedures, and they all produce similar results: Managerial sex typing in favor of men is a global phenomenon.[14] Sex typing, or associating desirable work characteristics to males over females, continues to be a barrier to female equality in the workplace.

Shein's initial study in the 1970s found that both female and male managers believed men were more likely to hold management characteristics than women. In a later study, she found that female managers are beginning to see women and men as equally likely to possess characteristics necessary for managerial success. This is encouraging and should mean that female managers would treat men and women similarly in hiring, placement, and promotion decisions.

There is some evidence in other industries that female managers treat men and women similarly in workplace assessments. One study involving Silicon Valley law firms showed female-founded firms provide more advancement

---

[14]Schein, V. E. (2001). A global look at psychological barriers to women's progress in management. *Journal of Social Issues, 57*(4), 675–688.

opportunities for women compared to firms where none of the founders were women.[15] In this study, there was also evidence of less pay inequality among lower-level employees reporting to a female, as opposed to those reporting to a male, manager.

Disappointingly, in Shein's replication studies, the male managers still held attitudes that reflected gender stereotypes. Despite all the societal, legal, and organizational changes that occurred over several decades between the studies, males continue to perceive males as more likely to possess successful managerial characteristics than females.

AFFINITY BIAS

When I work with the Women Advocacy Circles, I ask participants to list ten people they trust (not including family members). Next, I ask them to create columns next to the names and fill in the person's age, gender, race, and religion. When everyone is finished, they review their lists for similarities. I often hear a snicker or two. Most of the participants discover that the people they trust are similar in demographics and they look like themselves!

Aristotle wrote, "*Friends function as a kind of mirror of each other: insofar as friendship rests on similarity of character. In friendship, there is a mutuality of affection, sharing, concern and trust.*" Generally, we build trust with people who are like us. The experts call this "affinity bias," a type of unconscious bias which is part of the human condition.[16] It's a common phenomenon that occurs throughout our social networks from marriage and friendships to the people we have lunch with at work. Human beings feel more comfortable with people who share similar socio-demographic, intrapersonal, and behavioral characteristics.

Imagine the implications of affinity biases in management. What if you had a great job opportunity or project? Who would you select to work on the assignment with you? You may select an individual of your same gender without even realizing it.

At Westpac, affinity bias was observed in male managers who were more comfortable communicating with each other, especially in sales and service areas.[17] Client facing roles predominantly a male domain in the past remain stubborn to change. Although it is less overt than twenty years ago (since it is widely understood to be politically incorrect), the tendency to see males in these roles persists, especially among the older generation. Women at Westpac

[15] Beckman, C. M., & Phillips, D. J. (2005). Interorganizational determinants of promotion: Client leadership and the attainment of women attorneys. *American Sociological Review, 70*(4), 678–701.

[16] Annis, D. B. (1987). The meaning, value, and duties of friendship. *American Philosophical Quarterly, 24*(4), 349–356.

[17] Beck, D., & Davis, E. (2005). EEO in senior management: Women executives in Westpac. *Asia Pacific Journal of Human Resources, 43*(2), 273–288.

who complained about affinity bias conceded they found it difficult to create connections with males due to their dissimilarities and chalked it up to human nature.[18] Although this may be true, women need to be proactive in looking for ways to reduce affinity bias.

Mentor Insight: Go out of your way to find opportunities to connect with your male counterparts and male boss. Develop interests and look for commonalities to bypass gender differences and develop trusting relationships.

BARRIERS HAVE CONSEQUENCES

Upper management at financial service organizations is concerned about women in senior positions leaving their firms. At Westpac, many women in senior positions lamented how difficult it still was to break down the cultural barriers. After some time, they grow frustrated, tired, and eventually leave.[19] This phenomenon has been seen in other studies as well.

In a survey of 1000 financial professionals, 88% of the female financial service professionals indicated that gender discrimination existed within the industry. Many said they have seen it in their own firm and a third claimed experiencing discrimination personally.[20] Affinity bias is one type of discrimination causing discrepancies in promotion, recognition, and compensation.

Several class action lawsuits have alleged that older male advisors preparing to retire distribute their book of business to younger male advisors and not female advisors (due to affinity bias). These large books with wealthy clients provide higher compensation for the men and leave women holding the short end of the stick.

A study done by Mabel Abraham, from Columbia Business School, showed a similar phenomenon in entrepreneurial networking groups where the objective is to help each other generate new clients. Dr. Abraham found that women receive less leads from their colleagues because male entrepreneurs providing the leads assume clients prefer a man. Women in male-dominated occupations such as finance were the most penalized.[21]

These examples result in women receiving lower compensation. According to a study done by the Institute for Women's Policy, female financial advisors

[18]Beck, D., & Davis, E. (2005). EEO in senior management: Women executives in Westpac. *Asia Pacific Journal of Human Resources, 43*(2), 273–288.

[19]Beck, D., & Davis, E. (2005). EEO in senior management: Women executives in Westpac. *Asia Pacific Journal of Human Resources, 43*(2), 273–288.

[20]Tuttle, Beecher. 2014. How female bankers react to gender bias today. eFinancialCareers, http://news.enancialcareers.com/us-en/184541/female-bankers-recommend-gender-biased-rmwomen-colleagues/. Accessed March 6, 2017.

[21]Abraham, M. (2015, January). Explaining unequal returns to social capital among entrepreneurs. In *Academy of Management Proceedings* (Vol. 2015, No. 1, p. 11264). Academy of Management.

earn 56 cents on every dollar than male financial advisors earn.[22] The study looked at 120 occupations listed with Bureau of Labor Statistics. The institute found the largest pay gap in the financial services industry. If the pay gap was the result of women taking time off for child care, we would expect the pay gap to be uniform across all industries but the median pay gap for all full-time workers in this study was 82 cents on every dollar. Even female accountants earn 80 cents on the dollar. The difference in pay between male and female financial advisors, when other industries have narrowed the gap, underscores a clear problem that cannot be ignored.

Lower pay, less likelihood of promotion, and less job fulfillment compared to men are a clear explanation for why women vote with their feet. A study by the consulting firm, Mercer, called "When Women Thrive," found females in financial services management roles 20 to 30% more likely to leave their job than females in other industries.[23] One young female banker who was interviewed in the report said, "I came into my career in financial services with aspirations to make it to the top. But now, five years into it, I am planning my escape." This sentiment has been echoed in other studies.

Compare this to males in senior financial services roles who were more likely to stay in their position than males in other industries.[24] Women experience their financial careers differently than men. The career trade-off of lower expected benefits in terms of promotion, income, and recognition may not exceed the higher costs in terms of not fulfilling cultural expectations, deviating from social norms, and paying for child care. If the benefit does not exceed the cost, it is no wonder women decide to leave.

In Chapter 4, discussing beliefs and social pressure, I mention an Australian study showing women will seize upon opportunities to leave frustrating financial careers. The study infers that it is not the pull of the opportunity but instead the escape the opportunity provides. Carolyn Neck from the University of Queensland Brisbane, QLD, Australia, published this study highlighting frustration that causes women to exit senior financial roles.[25] Her insights derived from interviews debunk the notion that women are leaving due to work–life balance issues. Controlling for the plethora of variables such as marriage, children, education, and job experiences, she found these variables did

---

[22] https://iwpr.org/wp-content/uploads/2017/04/C456.pdf. The only other five occupations (out of 120 occupations) where gender earnings were less than 66% men's median weekly earnings were: insurance sales agent, physician and surgeon, real estate broker and sales agent, securities, commodities and financial services sales agents, and marketing and sales managers.

[23] https://www.mercer.com/our-thinking/when-women-thrive.html.

[24] http://www.oliverwyman.com/our-expertise/insights/2016/jun/women-in-financial-services-2016.html.

[25] Neck, C. (2015). Disappearing women: Why do women leave senior roles in finance? Further evidence. *Australian Journal of Management, 40*(3), 511–537.

not fully account for women leaving the profession.[26] The result suggests there are other determinants and that the often cited excuse for female under-representation (work–life balance) in financial services may be a red herring. Discussions focused on work–life balance detract from the more complicated and difficult explanations such as unconscious bias. The women interviewed in Neck's study spoke less about work–life issues and more about unsupportive corporate cultures. They were discouraged due to an unfriendly work environment that did not support skill development, participation in visible projects, or delegation of the assignments required for promotion.

At a recent CFP Board conference, a top executive from one of the major financial conglomerates, a man, spoke about the work his organization was doing to create better maternal and other work–life benefits. He said this was the key to helping women succeed. We have a lot of work to do if the men at the top think this predicament can be fixed solely by adopting family-friendly policies.

A *Harvard Business Review* article demonstrated the importance of recognizing that the challenge goes beyond work–life balance in order to rectify the problem. The article profiled Deloitte & Touche, one of the largest accounting, tax, and consulting firms in America and their efforts to address challenges women face in the workplace. Nine years earlier they recognized that although they had been actively recruiting women from colleges and business schools, female partners only accounted for 2% of the senior women.[27] Women were leaving the firm at significantly greater rates than men. The company assumed they were leaving due to the desire for work–life balance, which they couldn't control.

When Deloitte & Touche decided to dig deeper into the problem, they learned that women left because of the lack of opportunity in the firm's male-dominated culture. Deloitte listened and a cultural revolution, inspired from the top, drastically changed the company. The change led to greater creativity, faster growth, and far better performance for their clients, making the company's efforts well worth it.

The firm reduced their gender gap turnover from 25% in 1990 to less than 16% in 2011 saving the firm millions of dollars due to retention.[28] CEO Mike Cook set the tone from the top. People noticed when he cancelled his membership to a country club that excluded women.

When the firm created an environment of flexibility for everyone, turnover for all employees reduced by 50% in their critical consulting business and job

[26]Kark, R., & Eagly, A. H. (2010). Gender and leadership: Negotiating the labyrinth. In *Handbook of gender research in psychology* (pp. 443–468). New York: Springer.

[27]McCracken, D. M. (2000). Winning the talent war for women: Sometimes it takes a revolution. *Harvard Business Review, 78*(6), 159–167.

[28]https://www2.deloitte.com/content/dam/Deloitte/us/Documents/about-deloitte/us-inclusion-deloitte-numbers-support-gut-021913.pdf.

satisfaction improved by 25%. They cited research which shows people who work 60 flexible hours a week are happier than those who work 40 non-flexible hours. They argued that organizations that don't adapt to this fact will lose talent.[29] By creating a work culture which allows both men and women flexibility, the stigma associated with only mothers opting for flexible schedules was eliminated.

WORK–LIFE—EMBRACED
UNIVERSAL CULTURE OR RELUCTANT COMPROMISE

Recognition that work–life balance is an objective everyone strives for takes the focus off of women. Both women and men at various levels of management rank work–life balance in the top five personal challenges they face in their organizations.[30] In an Irish study, researchers from Dublin, Ireland, found the greatest obstacle to work–life balance was seen as the long hours and inflexibility in work options.[31] Using a questionnaire designed to get both female and male views, they found that both men and women in senior management would like to avail themselves to flexible arrangements but don't out of fear of jeopardizing their career.

More firms should consider Deloitte's approach in making flexible policy changes universal and culturally acceptable for everyone within their organization. Deloitte keeps their foot on the gas as they continue to be a leader in promoting women all over the world and continue to push for radical transformation of diversity and inclusion.[32] This grand scale effort permeating from the top is what financial service firms must employ if they truly want change.

The discussion of work–life balance is still a quagmire in many financial firms where widespread flexibility is not embraced. Marianne Bertrand from the University of Chicago and Lawrence Katz and Claudia Goldin from Harvard University studied MBAs who graduated between 1990 and 2006 from a top US business school. They found that although male and female MBAs started out with identical incomes, after ten years, male earnings significantly exceeded females.[33] Having children is the obvious reason that female

[29] https://www2.deloitte.com/content/dam/Deloitte/us/Documents/about-deloitte/us-inclusion-deloitte-numbers-support-gut-021913.pdf.

[30] Morley, K. (2004), 2004 Mt Eliza Leadership Index, Mt Eliza Centre for Executive Education, Melbourne Business School.

[31] Drew, E., & Murtagh, E. M. (2005). Work/life balance: Senior management champions or laggards? *Women in Management Review, 20*(4), 262–278.

[32] https://www2.deloitte.com/content/dam/Deloitte/us/Documents/about-deloitte/us-inclus-millennial-influence-120215.pdf.

[33] Bertrand, M., Goldin, C., & Katz, L. F. (2010). Dynamics of the gender gap for young professionals in the financial and corporate sectors. *American Economic Journal: Applied Economics, 2*(3), 228–255.

MBAs take time off from their careers when there are no flexible options offered. Although there is no evidence to suggest their productivity suffers upon returning to work, the penalty for taking time off or opting for reduced hours, when these choices result in discrimination, is enormous.[34] Bertand, Katz, and Goldin found female MBAs who took time off to have and raise children experienced reduced compensation but females in other professions such as physicians, PhDs, and lawyers did not suffer from this problem.

Claudia Goldin explores why the gender pay gap is larger in the finance profession than most other professions.[35] Her interest lies in the convergence of roles between men and women where they have similar productive capacities such as their education, professional degrees, and life cycle labor-force participation (how many years they been productive members of the workforce). She identifies the parent penalty as being a large factor in creating "wage-discrimination" between men and women.

Mentor Insight: If you take time off but think you want to reenter the workforce at a later point, look for a way to develop additional skills or at least maintaining current skills during the time you are away. The SWOT analysis presented in Chapter 7 can help you determine what skills, degrees, or certifications to focus on to make yourself more marketable and counteract the parent penalty for time away.

Goldin asserts that some industries such as the pharmaceutical industry, a high income, low "wage-discrimination" industry where women make up 55% of pharmacists, have restructured their work environment allowing for flexibility as the norm, not as an exception creating a stigma.[36] The finance industry lags behind this trend toward flexible adaptation. Women in finance receive a pay penalty for time gaps in their work history, which indicate a period of time where they were not productive members of the workforce. If their skills have truly suffered this might be fair but alternative ways to structure a flexible, team approach that will not impair wages should be explored.

Mentor Insight: While the finance industry makes attempts to restructure to allow for flexibility, you should consider this factor when determining the type of organization and business model you pursue. Keeping in mind your values, your beliefs and plans for the future can help you select the right organization and perhaps create your own flexibility by teaming up with another professional.

When exploring which organizations support work–life balance, caution should be applied. Even when firms offer opportunities for flexibility, the cultures at many firms are still tainted by unconscious bias and discrimination. Flexibility should be part of the culture where everyone can avail themselves,

[34]Goldin, C. (2014). A grand gender convergence: Its last chapter. *American Economic Review, 104*(4), 1091–1119.

[35]Ibid.

[36]Ibid.

not as an allowance which magnifies the neediness of an individual taking advantage of the firm's concession. Studies have shown that women are afraid to avail themselves to policies such as paternal leave or flextime because they believe that senior management will not approve.[37]

At Westpac, there is a perceived gap between the work–life balance rhetoric and reality. Employees at the firm have declared that when they took advantage of the benefits, comments from colleagues ranged from "you slept in" to "you've been laying by the pool." If someone chose to work from home, coworkers made comments such as, "oh, so you had a day off, did you?"[38] Women were lured into thinking they are still "players," but the minute they opted to take advantage of family-friendly benefits, they were written off as not committed or serious about their job.

Mentor Insight: Be aware that some people interpret a lack of visibility as a lack of commitment so it is good to communicate where you are and what you are working on when you are away from the office. In many financial institutions face time is still strategically important so when you are a mother you need to vigilant in making sure you are seen when others are there.

A recent 20-nation study showed that family-friendly policies such as long maternity leaves actually make the gender wage gap larger and reduced promotion opportunities for women even more.[39] The study showed that although maternal policies made it easier for women to work, they were more likely to work in non-managerial positions resulting in a gender earnings gap. In other words, with equivalent skills, women taking advantage of parental-friendly benefits earn less than women who don't avail themselves to these policies.

Discrimination might explain why family policies have been unsuccessful since those who utilize the policies are not promoted. In academia, the fear is being denied tenure.[40] A study at Penn State evaluated the success of their family-friendly program and showed that for a period of eight years, more than 500 faculty members became new parents, but only seven parental leaves were reported (and none by men).

Back when my children were young, I avoided the negative perception of motherhood by simply not telling people that I had children—which is extreme. I didn't place pictures of my children on my desk and I didn't talk

[37] Cross, C., linehan, M., & Murphy, C. (2017). The unintended consequences of role modelling behavior in female career progression. *Personnel Review, 46*(1).

[38] Beck, D., & Davis, E. (2005). EEO in senior management: Women executives in Westpac. *Asia Pacific Journal of Human Resources, 43*(2), 273–288.

[39] Mandel, H., & Semyonov, M. (2005). Family policies, wage structures, and gender gaps: Sources of earnings inequality in 20 countries. *American Sociological Review, 70*(6), 949–967.

[40] Drago, R., Colbeck, C. L., Stauffer, K. D., Pirretti, A., Burkum, K., Fazioli, J., ... & Habasevich, T. (2006). The avoidance of bias against caregiving: The case of academic faculty. *American Behavioral Scientist, 49*(9), 1222–1247.

about them. I made some sacrifices that I regret, but at the time, I thought it was what I had to do. I remember leaving my 10-year-old son home alone on a snow day because I didn't want anyone at work to know I had children and assume I was not capable of doing my work. Now, I realize I could have been more open while making my commitment to the company visible and playing up my strengths through my brand messaging.

PERCEPTION BECOMES REALITY

Susan worked hard and I valued her work tremendously. She was a new mother and had pictures of her beautiful daughter all over her desk. At lunch, she told funny stories about her daughter. She was in love and very proud. It was hard for her to come back to work after her maternity leave was over but she knew she wanted to work, she liked the intellectual stimulation, and she aspired to be in management.

Coincidentally, the plant manager, Jack, had a daughter who was born at the same hospital in Morristown, NJ, around the same time. Susan often asked Jack about his wife and daughter and how they were doing. She didn't realize that, even though she was communicating her warmth and nurturing side as a mother, some of her coworkers observed that she was indirectly communicating a lack of competence and commitment (more on that later).

When she came to me about putting her name in for a promotion as a commercial manager in purchasing, I told her I would absolutely go to bat for her. The plant manager, on the other hand, didn't think she was "up to the task." He didn't think she was reliable and questioned, "What happens if her daughter gets sick?" He never asked how the daughter was taken care of; he just assumed Susan could not and would not pull off the responsibilities of the position.

When Susan told me she was leaving, I wasn't surprised since I knew she was frustrated. When I told Jack, he wasn't surprised either since he understood she had family obligations which were more important. But when I told him that Warmer Lambert had hired her in their candy plant to be their cost accounting manager and this was a big loss for us, I noticed the combined expression on his face of surprise and concern. His perception of Susan was not accurate and we lost a good employee because of it.

Mentor Insight: Perceptions can be managed. I know how Susan felt about her children and she had every right to believe that people would respect her for who she was and what she contributed at work. However, it is important to manage perceptions through your brand messaging.

Experimental studies demonstrate the severe penalties women are confronted with in the workplace upon disclosure of motherhood status. Mothers are perceived to be less competent, less committed to their jobs, are less likely to be hired, and are penalized by $11,000 in starting salary recommendations as compared to non-mothers.[41] A Cornell University study found that, when presented with two identical job applicant résumés (one woman without children and the other with children), 84% of participants said they would hire the woman without children, and only 47% would hire the mother.[42]

Amy Cuddy from Harvard University and Susan Fiske from Princeton University found working moms tend to be stereotyped into two camps: homemakers who are warm but incompetent, or female professionals who are competent but cold. Their research found that when working women became mothers, they automatically traded their perceived competence for perceived warmth, but when men became fathers they maintained their perceived competence and gained warmth.

They also found that people had less interest in hiring, promoting, and educating working moms relative to working dads and childless employees.[43] However, compared to non-fathers, fathers are perceived to be significantly more committed to their jobs, are held to lower performance standards, allowed to be late more frequently, and are offered higher salaries. These results that find fathers, and even childless men, more committed to their work than mothers have been observed in various studies.[44]

Mentor Insights: If you think you are being discounted due to your maternal status try to refocus attention on your occupational contribution through your brand messaging. Continue to communicate your needs as much as possible but try to be sensitive to perceptions and try not to be overly demanding.

[41] Cuddy, A. J., Fiske, S. T., & Glick, P. (2004). When professionals become mothers, warmth doesn't cut the ice. *Journal of Social Issues, 60*(4), 701–718.

[42] "Creating a Family Friendly Department: 2006 Chairs and Deans Toolkit," UC Faculty Family Friendly Edge, University of California at Berkeley, http://ucfamilyedge.berkeley.edu. Accessed June 24, 2006.

[43] Cuddy, A. J., Fiske, S. T., & Glick, P. (2004). When professionals become mothers, warmth doesn't cut the ice. *Journal of Social Issues, 60*(4), 701–718.

[44] Fuegen, K., Biernat, M., Haines, E., & Deaux, K. (2004). Mothers and fathers in the workplace: How gender and parental status influence judgments of job-related competence. *Journal of Social Issues, 60*(4), 737–754.

EXERCISE: ENSURING WORK–LIFE BALANCE

Achieving work–life balance is important to having a fulfilling life and career. It's hard to juggle workplace responsibilities, family responsibilities, and rest and relaxation time. The following exercise will help you identify areas you need to work on to achieve better balance.

List the top five areas you spend your time and determine the percentage of time you spend in each activity.

1. _____
   _____
2. _____
   _____
3. _____
   _____
4. _____
   _____
5. _____
   _____

List the top five areas you *want to spend your time* and the percentage of time you want to spend on each activity.

1. _____
   _____
2. _____
   _____
3. _____
   _____
4. _____
   _____
5. _____
   _____

How closely are these lists aligned? What changes do you need to make to your life to become more aligned? These changes should become your top goals because if you don't achieve work–life balance, you will not be happy in life or at work. This is important; don't ignore it!

_____
_____
_____
_____
_____
_____
_____
_____

CHAPTER 7

The Gender Trap

I met a woman named Janet at a financial literacy conference where we were both speaking. She told me about her company and specifically, her frustration in not seeing many females promoted to branch manager. She told me about a woman at her company who wanted to get promoted and receive recognition for her contributions. Time and time again, she was overlooked while younger, less experienced men were promoted instead.

Janet went on to explain that this woman was on several committees and her dedication went way beyond the work that others did for the branch. She said her book, and ultimately her income, suffered because she tended to so many organizational issues. Management took advantage of her inclination to pitch in; they asked her to do a lot of the hard lifting and wanted her expertise and judgment, but they didn't reward her. She lamented, "I'm not sure if it was a deliberate sexism, but management really took advantage of this woman's skills."

As I listened, it was clear that the woman did not control her career. She was not consciously engaged. It is important to take on critical roles, but you want them to be strategic and highly visible projects. It sounded to me like the work this woman was doing was tedious busy work. Did this effort make her more visible to her direct management? Was she utilizing her strengths and contributing to high-value opportunities? Did she express her expectations to her boss? It is important to understand that working harder should ensure that management perceives you as a team player, instead of a workhorse. Extra work needs to translate to recognition.

I asked Janet if she knew the answers to these questions. She said, "Well yes, the woman complained to management that she was sick of being on all of these committees and said she didn't want to do it anymore." Her boss's response said it all. He said, "Oh well, there isn't anyone else to fill in for you. As you know, John is our top producer and he has too many clients. Ken

© The Author(s) 2018
L. Mattia, *Gender on Wall Street,*
https://doi.org/10.1007/978-3-319-75550-2_7

has already been assigned several important, high-level clients. We don't want John or Ken to get distracted by committee work. Their work is too important to the firm."

I told Janet that her friend was clearly being used and she needed to stop. The problem was how could she get out of the committee work but still be seen as a team player. She needed to find a critical assignment that was too important for management to say no to, even though they didn't want to lose her on the committee.

Whereas, John or Ken would say, "Listen, I have a big proposal to get in, so I cannot attend that committee meeting," it is expected that Janet, as a woman, would cooperate and pitch in where needed. It seems that management does not expect her to advocate for herself or the direction of her career. Her inability to speak up for herself and her work performance is directly related to many women's inability to negotiate a salary before being hired or negotiate work assignments or promotions during their careers. Women often fear they will be perceived as selfish. Men, on the other hand, seem to be in a constant state of negotiation.

Mentor Insight: Learning how to effectively advocate and negotiate for yourself is a requirement for success. Commit to learning this skill.

THE DOUBLE BIND

Women often find themselves compelled to go over and beyond to demonstrate their value. To cooperate and to do what is expected of them, even if it is not in their best interest, which leaves them in a double-bind situation. Women face a double bind in many aspects of society, but in particular, the economy. For example, gender norms still support women who choose to stay home in a traditional role, but are in conflict with their financial needs to support their families. This is especially the case for single mothers.

One of the biggest double binds is related to socially prescribed female characteristics, which are often limiting. Society assumes women are nurturing, cooperative, and supportive, all traits that are in conflict with the attributes associated with financial leadership positions. It is assumed that nurturers are not good at establishing control, requesting deliverables, enforcing rules, offering opposing ideas, or demanding excellence. When women exhibit such leadership characteristics, they are behaving in opposition of expectations and social norms. Therefore, men and women with traditional mind-sets are naturally somewhat suspicious of female leaders. Many people who might self-identify as liberal and open-minded hold conservative values without being aware of it (again, with unconscious bias).

As the global controller at a division of Mars, I was responsible for reporting the company's performance compared to the strategic plan, the operating plan, and the forecast. It was a difficult position since I was, in essence, reporting on how one or another department failed to deliver what they initially promised. I always tried to make my presentations impersonal and stuck to the facts, but I was still the only woman in the room. On the one hand, the President, David, wanted the facts and demanded that of me, but on the other hand, I was told that I was confrontational by some of the management team members.

One time, I had to report on a significant shortfall in production, which was due to a broken machine. The engineers were struggling to fix it and couldn't seem to resolve the issue. The VP of Manufacturing, Allen, got up and started yelling at me. "How dare you criticize the engineering team! Who do you think you are? Do you think you could do any better?"

I assured him that I was not criticizing his team; I was identifying the shortfall. I said, "if we recognize the problem, there are several solutions. One option is to shift production to our manufacturing plant in Winnersh, England. At minimum the sales department needs to communicate pending late delivery to key customers." He didn't care what I said and was really annoyed that I dared to expose him.

Finally, David stepped in and told Allen that he was out of line. It was interesting to me because clearly, the president was protecting me from the big bully, as if he were my father. I both wanted the protection and was insulted by it. Reporting weaknesses in the operation was a hard thing to do, especially when gender norms said I should be nurturing and supportive.

Allen was a key stakeholder and I needed to make an effort to meet his needs. Over the next couple of months, I spoke to Allen prior to management meetings to collaborate on how to present the monthly results, which took the sting out. We partnered on how to position the information so that it demonstrated that he was in control. The results to the company were the same—the issues were identified and solutions were explored—but I had turned an enemy into an ally.

Mentor Insights: Get others invested in your career such as your boss and key stakeholders of the firm. Men do this naturally. Talk to stakeholders before the meeting to gain buy-in and/or understand possible criticisms. Don't go into a meeting cold. Make sure you are prepared to couch your points in a way that lets your stakeholders know you have considered their input.

There is a caveat, however. I relinquished being perceived as tough and demanding, characteristics associated with being a successful controller. Although I remained effective, my agency suffered, which was a compromise I had to accept. It was important to understand what the environment necessitated and what I needed to do to be successful.

This scenario was a perfect example of the double bind. I was walking the tight rope between being supportive and being authoritative. In my annual review, David told me that I went into the wrong profession. He said I should have become a nurse. Yet, Allen told me that I didn't stand for anything and that I needed to stand for something. Even their feedback was contradictory!

Mentor Insight: Learning how to exercise agency while not offending those tied to old-fashioned stereotypes can be tricky. Several techniques include prefacing your comments with your concern for others, the firm, etc., being sensitive to your tone and the pace of your words, using humor if it comes naturally for you and maintaining composure while you express yourself assertively (not passively or aggressively. See Chapter 13.)

Rutgers University conducted an experiment to demonstrate the double-bind problem for women who strive for leadership positions.[1] In the experiment, students were asked to make leadership hiring decisions based on an applicant's video. They deemed the female applicants who seemed competent and forceful to be in violation of feminine niceness. However, if the female applicant came across as too communal or supportive, she was not thought to be well suited for the job either. In both cases, the women were disqualified due to a lack of respect or because they were not liked.

If women are able to position their brand message as competent, but nice, perhaps they could avoid the backlash of negative perceptions since it seems that it is the forceful characteristic that creates the greatest offense. Some research suggests that a participatory style is less likely to receive negative evaluations, compared to those who have an autocratic, directive style.

A study by the Center for Work/Life Law at Hastings University examined women's various experiences in a focus group setting. The idea of the double bind resonated with much of the group.[2] The women felt they were often under-recognized and did not get adequate support. They were afraid to say anything for fear of being seen as a problem or too aggressive. Instead, they opted to remain compliant and be a "good girl" for fear of being labeled a "bitch."

Mentor Insight: Females tend to be the most likeable when they communicate both niceness and competence, but this is not necessarily so easy. It requires a delicate balance between displaying ability and ambition but not dominance or competitiveness. Attaining this judicious equilibrium requires practice and concious engagement which can earn the respect and influence necessary to achieve success.

If I had to identify the biggest challenge I have faced in the finance industry, it is walking this fine restrained and diplomatic line. At times, the effort has created self-doubt and anxiety about how to communicate—both of which are deterrents that have sent many women looking for an alternative career. The double bind is a hurdle that women have to deal with and yes, it is unfair we have to turn ourselves into a pretzel. There were times, I decided it was simply too hard to navigate what I said, how I acted and how others perceived

[1] Rudman, L. A., & Glick, P. (2001). Prescriptive gender stereotypes and backlash toward agentic women. *Journal of Social Issues, 57*(4), 743–762.

[2] Huang, P. (2008). *Gender bias in academia: Findings from focus groups.* San Francisco, CA: Center for WorkLife Law.

me. Instead, I focused on getting the job done even if I ruffled a few feathers. It was a mistake and now, I slow down and take the time to think about how I come across.

DIFFERENT STANDARDS

A recent study showed how females are held to different, more stringent standards than males. The study included all financial services employees registered with the Financial Industry Regulatory Authority (FINRA) from 2005 to 2015. In observing the data, the researcher found that, although 75% of the industry is male, female advisors are punished more often and more severely for misconduct on the job.[3]

This study also showed that female advisor misconduct is less costly, less risky, and less likely to be repeated than a male offense. Male advisors misconduct costs businesses 20% more than female misconduct. One in eleven male advisors has a record of past misconduct, compared to only one in thirty female advisors, which means that males are three times more likely to commit an offense. Ironically, female advisors are more likely to lose their job due to misconduct, less likely to be promoted, experience a longer unemployment as a result, and are 30% less likely to find a job in financial services compared to males.

In trying to explain why women are treated more unfairly than males, this scientific study controlled for variables such as assets under management (AUM) of advisors and other measures of productivity, which did not explain the difference in treatment. The most telling part is that the discrimination came from the employer—top management—which was primarily male, where the percentage of misconduct complaints were much higher for women than for men. Compare that to customer complaints, which are much higher for male advisors than female advisors.

Another example of unequal standards is relative to how executives are perceived when displaying emotions. There are times when leaders naturally become stressed or angry, when the organization hit roadblocks or experienced some type of difficulty. Because of the burden of responsibility, leaders naturally react to adverse news through an emotional display. It has been shown that men have more leeway in displaying anger than women. The research shows that anger expressed by men in a professional context confers a higher status but angry females are attributed a lower status. In fact, it doesn't matter if the female is a trainee or a CEO; they both received a lower status ranking.[4] The assumption is that the male leader is reacting to the external circumstances but the female leader is an angry person or is out of control, her reactions are attributed to internal characteristics.

[3] Egan, M. L., Matvos, G., & Seru, A. (2017). *When Harry fired Sally: The double standard in punishing misconduct* (No. w23242). National Bureau of Economic Research.

[4] Brescoll, V. L., & Uhlmann, E. L. (2008). Can an angry woman get ahead? Status conferral, gender, and expression of emotion in the workplace. *Psychological Science, 19*(3), 268–275.

Mentor Insight: Women who might use anger to compel people to fulfill responsibilities need to understand that maintaining an unemotional posture—will result in greater credibility and locus of control. Alternatively, communicating an external source for the anger can minimize gender bias.

Most women want to be evaluated on merit. It is often assumed in a competitive setting, where it is all about the bottom line, that meritocracy will prevail. The problem is that merit is not always easy to appraise. Even over time, if equal support structures are not in place, it is hard to know if outcomes are due to the quality of the individual or the quality of the processes used to support the individual.

When quality is uncertain and difficult to gauge or information is missing, evaluators default to heuristics such as gender. Even when information on quality is available, people still often rely on gender as an indicator for performance.

A recent field-based study by Tristan Botelho and Mabel Abraham explored gender bias and how it manifests in online evaluations of advisors providing stock recommendations. Dr. Botelho had previously worked in the investment banking industry and had observed illogical gender preferences prompting interest in learning if gender bias was statistically significant in the financial industry. Using data from a private knowledge-sharing platform, Bothelho and Abraham observed that evaluators would ignore the recommendations that yielded the highest return and instead used the gender of the advisor to rank the performance of the advisor. Men received higher performance evaluations where average-quality men received the benefit of the doubt but women had to be super stars (in the top 10%) to receive similar evaluations.[5] Women were held to a higher standard of evaluation.

These different standards between men and women affect hiring, promotions, pay, job assignment, and overall job satisfaction. Sex-biased hiring is hard to prove but one study used "blind auditions" to evaluate candidates to join a symphony orchestra. Researchers found that hiding the candidate behind a screen increased the probability of females being hired.[6] Even my fifteen-year-old daughter's symphony has adopted blind auditions. Financial firms may consider using similar blind hiring processes although it could be difficult to implement.

Mentor Insight: When selecting a firm, look for policies on gender blind hiring and evaluation processes. A way to detect a female-friendly firm is one where women are in the higher ranks, either as a founder or as a managing director. Of course, this does not guarantee an equitable work experience but the data suggest the odds are more in your favor.

[5] Botelho, T. L., & Abraham, M. (2017). Pursuing quality: How search costs and uncertainty magnify gender-based double standards in a multistage evaluation process. *Administrative Science Quarterly.* https://doi.org/10.1177/0001839217694358.

[6] Goldin, C., & Cecilia, R. (2000). Orchestrating impartiality: The impact of blind auditions on female musicians. *American Economic Review, 90*(4), 715–741.

It Is Not About You. It Is About Your Gender

If women don't recognize gender bias, there is a danger that they might accept as fact that they are under-performers. In 2005, at a National Bureau of Economic Research luncheon, Lawrence Summers, then-president of Harvard University, said that "aptitude" is the second most significant reason that women don't tend to excel in math and science. While acknowledging that there is discrimination against women in the scientific workplace, Summers said outright that women are less willing than men to make professional sacrifices and that men have more innate ability than women for high-level analytical work. Talk about bias!

Many female scientists were furious, and several scientists said there is no empirical evidence to support Summers' statements. Dr. Ben Barres of the Stanford University School of Medicine responded with an article in the prestigious journal, *Nature*, citing statistics pointing to discrimination as the key cause of differences between men and women in science careers.

There is abundant evidence that social constructionism and gender-role socialization has impeded women's progress in analytical careers. Women need to recognize that they are capable of analytical endeavors and have an inherent ability to understand money. Female role models in financial services can help with this cause.

Mentor Insight: Only you really know what you are capable of—listen to your own instincts. Some people may only see your gender and make assumptions. It is important that you are brutally honest with yourself and make certain you know your strengths. Don't let anyone create doubt or make you second-guess yourself. If you think your competence is in question, nip it in the bud. Be prepared, perhaps even over prepared.

SET UP FOR FAILURE

Differences in the quality of job assignments women receive reveal further gender discrimination. Women often find themselves with relatively riskier and less desirable assignments than men. One study showed that some of the largest public companies are more likely to hire females in leadership roles if the company had experienced bad performance in the preceding 5 months.[7] The situation puts women in more precarious situations where they are exposed to criticism and in danger of being blamed for the bad performance.

My position as the CFO for a strategic business unit at Telcordia Technologies was a case in point. Telcordia Technologies was a company that came out of the 1982 decentralization of the Bell System and received the name of Bell Communications Research, nicknamed Bellcore. It was a consortium

---

[7] Ryan, M. K., & Haslam, S. A. (2005). The glass cliff: Evidence that women are over-represented in precarious leadership positions. *British Journal of Management, 16*(2), 81–90.

established by the Regional Bell Operating Companies (RBOCs) upon their separation from AT&T so that the operating companies were able to maintain a shared research and development facility.

The firm was full of really smart scientists who invented much of the telecommunication functionality we enjoy today such as caller ID, call waiting, mobile number portability, and toll-free telephone numbers. Since it was the research arm for the RBOCs, it was essentially a cost center, which means the scientists would work on whatever cool ideas they had and at the end of the month split the bill among the seven Regional Holding companies that divested from the AT&T system.

I was hired in 1999, after Science Applications International Corporation (SAIC) acquired the company and mandated its transition from a cost center to a profit center. Out of the four strategic business units (SBU), the one having the most trouble with the transition was the professional services group, which consisted of all the true inventors (think-tank types) who were more interested in technological advances than they were in the idea of generating a profit.

Guess which SBU hired me; a woman and the only woman at this level? Me! And no wonder; the challenge was huge. Convincing these scientists, they needed internal controls, spending approvals, forecasts, and budgets, was not an easy task. They had never been constrained by these types of limitations before. Essentially, I was tasked with changing the culture of the business after the man originally assigned to the job had failed.

I stayed at the company for three years. During that time, I worked ten-hour days, established all the processes needed to be a commercial organization, and then sold it to the seven business unit groups. It was challenging, I learned a lot but I also now know that I got the job because it was not a desirable position. Most men would not have taken it.

Define Your Strengths

I met Vanessa at Geller and Company. She was a controller on various client assignments. A top performer and a great supporter of the company, she was very good at her job and the clients loved her. However, she was viewed as someone who was well placed and not promotable. One day, we were on a client assignment and I told her how much I appreciated her work. "That is nice," she said, "but I really want to be promoted to CFO, and I don't see that ever happening."

After discussing her strengths with her, we both agreed that she had great technical skills but had not displayed soft skills such as business development, diplomacy when giving bad news to a client CEO, or motivating the team when the work became onerous. We decided to develop a plan so she could overcome this weakness. First, we agreed that I would recommend for her to receive a personal coach so she could work on these skills. We also agreed that she would take over one of the easier client relationships to get more experience, practice, and exposure. Understanding her strengths and weaknesses in the context of her next promotion was an important step in realizing her vision for her career.

Mentor Insight: Identify the position or role you aspire to attain and then identify the characteristics and skills which will help you be successful in that role. Do this even before you actually get the job.

Reflecting back on my own experience as the cost accounting manager at M&M/Mars, I realize that what saved me was my ability to highlight my strengths quickly. I now understand I was in a gender trap where my credibility was being threatened. Rather than letting it deter me, I chose to focus on promoting my strengths and looked for opportunities to demonstrate my technical competence.

I worked on a project that had the potential to make a large impact on the company and increase my visibility. I didn't have to fight anyone for it since no one else identified the opportunity or possessed the required competencies.

Mentor Insight: Even if everyone welcomes you with open arms, you don't have a long honeymoon period in a new job. You need to get to work to establish your reputation and value early on or you will be digging yourself out of a hole for the rest of your career. Don't take too long to figure out the spots where you can add value. Get to work.

In the introduction of this book, I mentioned the scrap report. That report was the bane of the plant; every month, it showed all the materials that were lost and unaccounted for. Imagine that the plant lost large amounts of raw materials: sugar, cocoa, cocoa butter, etc., every month which no one could explain. The amount of loss was derived by taking a physical inventory of all the raw materials, work-in-process, and finished product at the end of the month and subtracting out what those inventory numbers were at the beginning of the month along with the materials used for sold product, to determine what was missing.

As a new MBA, I knew this process was archaic and went to speak to Brian, the head of the supply chain process. Coincidentally, he was interested in implementing a material requirements planning program (MRP), which is a production planning, scheduling, and inventory control system used to manage a manufacturing company's supply chain process from purchasing materials to manufacturing and all the way to customer delivery. This system would help many facets of the business. I explained that I could also use the system to implement better controls around the manufacturing process in the plant and particularly identify how raw materials were deployed. After having difficulty in assembling a team to change the process (most people don't like change), Brian was happy to let me participate and lead the charge in the plant.

Mentor Insight: Finding ways to add value while satisfying a stakeholder's objective is a win-win since you can shine from your own accomplishment while at the same time earn an advocate and supporter. You solved their problem.

I worked hard to implement the manufacturing changes. I knew once everyone saw what the system and related process adjustments could do, they would support the change. In the end, my work saved money and time and it identified the source of problems in the manufacturing process, making everyone's job easier. Everyone—yes, even Dana—was impressed. I not only got the work done but I was able to sell it across the business to gain cooperation and buy-in. I was asked to help the other six plants in the USA and the plant in Toronto, Canada, implement the same system and processes. My work spoke for itself, and the recognition I received set the stage for a promotion.

Take note that I was not offered this assignment. Most of my colleagues and superiors in financial management did not appreciate or value the knowledge gained by working as a cost accountant or fraternizing with plant workers and being immersed in the operational process. In fact, many accountants and financial analysts avoid cost accounting because it is less visible and physically remote from the CFO office. That is exactly what made the role so appealing to me. I wanted to understand how the proverbial "sausage" was made. Knowledge was power. Once I had the power, I was able to provide value. No one intended to give me a mission-critical position. I took it and staked a claim. Fortunately, I was the only person who took the time to invest in the knowledge, develop a vision, and take the initiative to implement change.

Mentor Insight: Treat your career strategically. If you look around, you will see many opportunities to improve your business—there are always plenty of areas that need improvement. An ideal situation is one that capitalizes on your strengths, satisfies a true business need, and doesn't put you in competition with your colleagues.

Keep in mind that you are not alone. Management is at least partially invested in helping you because they hired you for the position. They might volunteer to advocate for you and become your "sponsor," but sometimes you need to prod them along. Use your annual review to promote your work and your aspirations. Let your boss know what you want and are willing to do. For example, if you're willing to take an international assignment, let your manager know. Find out if there is a formal leadership development program, a coaching program, or an advocacy circle program (more on that in Chapter 12) available at your firm. If there is a cost and you can convince your boss to pay for the program, he/she will be even further invested in your success.

Mentor Insight: Enroll your management team and get your boss to help you create a plan based on your strengths and the opportunities you've identified. Make certain he/she sees the value of your proposed contribution. Understand your boss has some stake in your success, especially if it also makes him/her look good and advances the organization's goals.

Exercise: Positioning Strengths in Your Current Environment (SWOT Analysis)

As a member of the management team at various corporations and small businesses, once a year we reviewed our vision, mission, strategic priorities, and what we needed to do to put our vision in motion. SWOT is a key analysis tool to identify the corporation's Strengths, Weaknesses, Opportunities, and Threats. It is also an effective tool to create your own personal strategy.

Strengths: The skills, competencies, and abilities that make you exceptional for a career in personal financial advising.

_____
_____
_____
_____
_____
_____
_____

Weaknesses: What do you need to work on to get you where you want to go? Consider positions you would like to be promoted into and identify the technical and soft skills that you lack to get there. Business relationships should also be considered in this review.

_____
_____
_____
_____
_____
_____
_____

Opportunities: What you can do to make an impact at your firm? Take a good look around at the areas that can be improved. How can you apply your strengths to implement improvements? Look for the biggest improvement that will give you the most visibility. Usually, management is so thankful that someone has taken an initiative that at worst, they will be grateful for the improved situation, and at best, you may get what you want—perhaps that promotion.

_____
_____
_____
_____
_____
_____

Threats: As an optimist, I prefer to ignore threats, but as a realist, it is important to be aware of potential hurdles that could block success. There are many
threats that don't originate from gender such as budget cuts, mergers, health,
or outsourcing. There are also gender-related threats. Some of these threats
are bigger than others, so you need to identify which ones could impact you.

_____
_____
_____
_____
_____
_____

Reflection: Are you in the right environment, where you are able to use your
strengths to capture opportunities? What needs to change?

_____
_____
_____
_____
_____
_____

CHAPTER 8

The Pain of Isolation

Carol, a CFA®, worked at a large Wall Street bank, surrounded by smart, funny, and like-minded people. She started investing in the stock market when she was 14 years old and loves the world of investing. She told me how fortunate she felt to be working with equity investing. It was her favorite subject matter; she reads and talks about the markets even during her free time. Her job was challenging and fulfilling, but she started to be less and less interested in going to work and she became increasingly depressed.

After trying to pinpoint the reasons for her depression and her desire to pull back, Carol admitted some of her frustrations. "I am the only female there and the men are not interested in my stories or conversation. They just want to talk about sports and girls and some of the things they talk about are disgusting, but I don't engage or say anything, so they think they can carry on. I'm not going to report them to HR. I just want nothing to do with them. And I'm shy and introverted too, so the idea of trying to forge new relationships scares me to death, even if I know it would be for my own good."

The result was that Carol felt almost entirely alone at work. She didn't have anyone to discuss what was happening at home or the latest political events with. "But no one bothers me either. I just do my work, and I think they respect my analytical capabilities enough that people don't challenge my decisions. I guess I should just be happy since I am paid well and everything is fine." Carol's isolation did not impede her ability to perform or her compensation, but it led to a less than enjoyable work–life.

Mentor Insight: To fight isolation, women need to call on natural abilities to build relationships. This natural ability can give them a competitive advantage as financial advisors. But many women are unable to tap into these abilities to develop relationships for the purpose of excelling in the workplace, particularly when most of the co-workers are male. Females interested in working in fields

L. Mattia, *Gender on Wall Street*,
https://doi.org/10.1007/978-3-319-75550-2_8

which have traditionally been male-dominated (such as finance) need to proactively strategize on how to kindle their innate relationship-building skills.

Hakan Ozcelik, from California State University, and Sigal Barsade, from the Wharton School of Business, studied loneliness in the workplace. After surveying a sample of 672 workers, they concluded that loneliness at work affected performance on both direct tasks and team effectiveness.[1] They also concluded that it was not an individual problem; management needed to address it as an organizational problem. While there are a variety of reasons why an individual would feel lonely, feeling excluded due to gender is a big problem.

BELONGINGNESS

If a Wall Street executive is expected to be a man, then a woman is second choice; she doesn't really "belong." That is how I felt working at Geller and Company as the only female CFO among nine CFO/managers and our managing director, Jack. I didn't realize that Jack had hired me with the intention that I be part of his succession plan. When Bill, one of the other CFOs, got wind of it, he became my enemy and looked for every chance to undermine me. By this point in my career, I knew how to deal with Bill. After Dana, I could deal with anyone.

I focused on my work and built a book of fifteen early-stage NYC firms. Working as their part-time CFO, I was billing at $325 an hour. I had teams of controllers, bookkeepers, and analysts who I brought in. Since each firm was at a different stage of their development, they all had unique needs, which meant it was inefficient for these new businesses to hire a staff of varied expertise. For example, one firm was gearing up for an IPO, so they needed specialized SEC expertise, where another firm was looking for venture capitalist funding and needed to develop their business case, which required business analysis and planning work. The teams I used for each client were very different.

Bill was an integral team member and leader at Geller and he'd been there for six years. It was clear that he thought he should be the successor when Jack moved on. I was the newest member, a female, and a potential threat—not a recipe for inclusion. Bill would make certain I was not invited to any of their informal social events. He and the rest of the guys often went out to lunch or for drinks after work. They joked in the office and shared war stories. My boss supported me and I spent time exchanging ideas with him, the other staff, and my clients but I wasn't part of the team of CFOs. I like being part of a team so this made my job much less enjoyable.

[1] Ozcelik, H., & Barsade, S. (2011, January). Work loneliness and employee performance. In *Academy of Management Proceedings* (Vol. 2011, No. 1, pp. 1–6). Academy of Management.

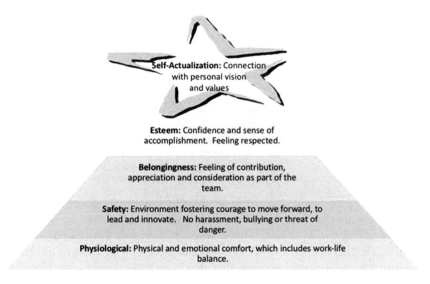

Fig. 8.1 Maslow's hierarchy of needs in the workplace

Social isolation creates an environment in which women are unsure how to establish themselves as competent colleagues, worthy of inclusion. In my case, it created an unfriendly environment. I didn't to go to our office on the Upper East Side of Manhattan and arranged to do all my work at a client's office.

I decided to leave the firm for several reasons, but it didn't help that I never developed a sense of belonging. Belongingness is important for engagement, which motivates us to come back to work every day.

Studying psychology, we learned about belongingness and how it is a key building block to achieving life satisfaction. We studied Dr. Abraham Maslow's motivation theory and his hierarchy of human needs. I will never forget the five-tier model of human needs, depicted as hierarchical levels within a pyramid.

Maslow's hierarchy can be used to illustrate the type of work environment required to cultivate a financial star (see Fig. 8.1). After meeting basic physiological and safety needs, including work–life balance and a bully-free environment, all humans need to feel they belong. If they don't feel they belong, the confidence to gain a healthy self-esteem is threatened and the value alignment/self-actualization required to become a financial star is compromised. Without a sense of belonging, there is no way to feel fully satisfied in a job and to become the top quality performer, a star-bound financial advisor strives to become.

There is sufficient literature on the idea that women in the STEM fields—science, technology, engineering, and math—have social difficulty. It seems that finance might be a cousin to these STEM fields. One study of women in the workplace found that both men and women were less likely to discuss research with female colleagues as opposed to male colleagues because of stereotypes that women are less knowledgeable.[2] While discussions about women's sense of belonging on a social level ensue, these results imply that women are less apt to interact with men even when it is related to work.

Mentor Insight: When making a decision about a job, it is important to consider if you feel like you belong there. Is the environment and the situation conducive for you to get along with your co-workers and be part of the team?

CHOOSE TO BELONG

The study by Penelope Huang from the Center of Worklife Law found a recurring theme that women did not fit in and were often left out of informal activities in the work setting.[3] Even when the omission was unintentional, it still made the women in the study feel detached from the group. Huang found that some women indicated that they didn't necessarily want to participate in the team activities. She quotes one member of a focus group as saying:

> One of the things about me is that I'm not very visible when I go to meetings. I don't go out to the bars and socialize and I don't know many of these people intimately that are in my field. ... I'm going to need letters of recommendation from the leaders in my field for tenure, but it's actually very hard for me to make the effort to go out and get to know the (mostly men) in my field so I can get these letters, which our director has indicated are really important. It's very hard for a woman to just go and join this group of men.

Mentor Insight: The first step to belonging is simply choosing to make an effort to be part of the team. Choosing not to participate ensures you will remain in isolation and you will not have the support you will inevitably need in the future. This is a big mistake.

As part of the management team, headquartered in the US, I went out of my way to develop relationships with the staff at the Winnersh England facility, especially with Paul, the plant manager of the plant and a key stakeholder. One afternoon, I asked Paul if we could go to the pub for a pint after work. This was what all the guys did. In fact, they often went out for a pint at lunch, but I don't know how they functioned for the rest of the afternoon.

Mentor Insight: Communicate with your colleagues and consider it an important aspect of your job. Learn to communicate effectively, build rapport with you colleagues and learn to negotiate and advocate your value.

[2] Holleran, S. E., Whitehead, J., Schmader, T., & Mehl, M. R. (2011). Talking shop and shooting the breeze: A study of workplace conversation and job disengagement among STEM faculty. *Social Psychological and Personality Science, 2*(1), 65–71.

[3] Huang, P. (2008). Gender bias in academia: Findings from focus groups. San Francisco, CA: Center for WorkLife Law.

Paul agreed and we went out to the local pub. Before I knew it, he was making a move on me.

I asked Paul why he thought it was appropriate and he said that women don't usually ask him out unless they're interested. "Paul!" I exclaimed, "I am the global controller. You are the plant manager. Doesn't it seem appropriate for us to develop a good relationship?" He said, "Yes, in most cases that is true but not when one of the parties is a girl." In the end, we managed to develop a working relationship but we didn't go out to the pub again, unless it was a large team outing.

Mentor Insight: This is the exact situation that many women fear. Many of us fear going up to a group of men at a conference and spending time with the men in social situations in fear of being mislabeled as loose, a party girl, or some other disparaging label. But we need to get past this if we want to "belong" in their world. If the situation becomes awkward, keep your composure and be matter-of-fact in correcting the perception.

Perhaps I was a bit naive to think I could just go out with Paul as one of the blokes. There was no way he would see *me* that way. I rushed and pushed too quickly. Perhaps later, when he was clear on what I stood for, it could have worked. Still, I found opportunities to socialize with him in the larger group where there was no ambiguity about my intention.

Mentor Insight: Take the relationship building slow when uncertain. This is new territory for both men and women. Look for natural opportunities to engage in the relationship and/or look for group activities that don't make things awkward.

GO WITH THE FLOW AND PARTICIPATE

A few years later in the same role at Mars, I partnered with the Global Commercial Manager, Rod, to identify a site to build a plant in Querétaro, Mexico. Querétaro City is the host for major corporations and is a strong business and economic center but it's still a little behind the times. I spent time in both Queretaro and Mexico City where I met with bankers and other vendors to help us with the plant. Often, I would find myself at a restaurant with a group of men. In fact, often the entire restaurant was filled with men. The only other females were taking care of us. The men weren't always certain how to include me, but I was the customer, so they were courteous and respectful.

In a celebration of the plant opening, the plant controller who I had hired, Juan, suggested that the group (all men again) go outside to smoke a cigar, which was a common activity in Mexico. I hesitated, but Juan nodded and gave me a respectful look as if to say, "you need to be part of this ritual." When Juan handed me a cigar, I took it and held it. I didn't smoke it (the thought makes me nauseous), but I held it the entire time the group spoke animatedly outside. I felt indebted to Juan because he went out of his way to show me respect and consideration. No one seemed shocked and they all went with the flow, acknowledging it was unusual but acceptable. That was all I could ask.

Mentor Insight: It is important to go with the flow and to participate in customs and activities that may be uncomfortable. If everyone is going to the bar, you should go too. You don't have to drink anything but you don't want to look out of place. I will admit that I have been known to pay bartenders to give me water with an olive in a martini glass. This way, I am part of the team but I didn't have to consume something I didn't want to consume.

Julie, a woman who I mentored, told me about how the guys at her office would go for coffee at the local Starbucks. Although everyone was invited, she didn't feel like she could afford to go because she had too much work. I convinced her that showing up to these coffee meetings may be the most important part of her job.

Reluctantly, she began to go out for coffee with the guys from the office. She was the only woman in the group. They talked about football and what happened over the weekend, but they also talked about things going on in the department. These men were all in the know.

One afternoon, Julie called me and said, "I did what you suggested. I had coffee with the guys this morning and I am so glad that I did. There was all of this discussion about funding and they said the firm is looking for a new manager for our department. It was important stuff! They discussed who had applied and what the company was expecting from the next in line and they detailed the overall succession plan." Julie could not believe she would have never heard this stuff if she didn't go to Starbucks.

The guys were not purposefully excluding her (or anyone else) from their conversations. It's just that none of the women are showing up. They were all missing out on what was really happening.

Mentor Insight: Social isolation is a final pattern that can make it harder for women to "know the ropes" so that they can do what they need to do to be seen as competent.

Yes, it is true that men and women often have different interests. Maybe you feel like you shouldn't be forced to drink beer or listen to stories about football or fishing. There are consequences to not participating; primarily, being left out!

See Chapter 13 for help to connect with your colleagues. The following exercise will help you identify the key stakeholders who you must connect with to help you achieve success.

Exercise—Identifying Your Partners for Success (Stakeholder Analysis)

The first time I was introduced to a stakeholder analysis was when I began to learn how to implement effective business change at Telcordia Technologies. I was creating processes designed to change the organization from a cost center to a profit center; a major 360-degree change. I asked myself, "How can I influence a diverse group of people so they would support the change?" and stumbled upon this technique.

Change is hard. Everyone has their own agenda and their own reasons for not wanting change. Alas, the objective of this exercise is to help each of them see how the change can benefit them and address the concerns they have in their job. It goes back to the old, "What's in It for Me (WIFM)?" principal, which recognizes that most of us are primarily concerned with how change will influence our own personal lives.

Your goal is to get all the stakeholders (they can be a person or a group), including the unsupportive ones, to become advocates for your success. To do this, complete the following steps:

1. Create a list of all the stakeholders essential for your success.
   Identify the person who represents the voice of the group.
   - Identify the issues/concerns that are important to that person or group.
   - Establish what this person/group wants from you to support their issue/concern (consistent with what you are willing and able to do).
2. Once you have created this concern/win matrix, prioritize each stakeholder by identifying their level of influence and their level of interest in you and the work that you are doing by categorizing them as one of the following;
   Key player
   - Influencer
   - Engaged/Interested
   - No influence/low interest.

You should focus on meeting the needs of the key player or influencers and manage them closely. For the engaged/interested, you should try to show consideration and understanding of their concerns but spend less time meeting their needs. You should spend the least amount of time on those categorized as no influence/low interest. Identifying key players is critical for you to succeed. They have a high political interest and are powerful enough to support you in your success, promote you, or even have you fired. This analysis should be reviewed on a regular basis to track changes (real or perceived) in stakeholder attitudes. It should then be used to help you execute your plan.

EXAMPLE STAKEHOLDER ANALYSIS

Stakeholder	Person	Issues/concerns	Win
Immediate boss	Jack Smith	Clients leaving due to poor investment performance related to the market	Communication plan to speak and reassure the clients of the organization and the advisor value
Managing director/owner	John Davenport	Overall lack of cooperation and teamwork has cost the business clients and inefficiencies resulting in increased costs. Most concerned about firm's reputation	Development and communication of the strategic plan and priorities, which are included in each person's list of goals
Top advisors at the firm	Bob Stuart Carol Abrams	Investment committee not communicating their strategy. Perhaps they don't have one?	Weekly or monthly meetings, either by phone or in-person where the advisors could ask questions about investment choices that they see in client portfolios
Office manager	Rosie Cantor	Inefficiencies and lack of cooperation, where organization members seem to have lost respect for processes	Demonstration that individuals are adhering to the office rules and processes, trying their best to comply
Chief investment officer	Tim McDougal	Uncertain if the rest of the firm understands the value that his team produces for the firm, even in a bad market, they are producing alpha and no one even acknowledges their work	Receiving positive feedback from the owner and from the top advisors instead of usual negative comments

YOUR STAKEHOLDER ANALYSIS

Stakeholder	Person	Issues/concerns	Win

CHAPTER 9

The Fragility of the Female Network

The Waco, Texas plant manager at Mars was a woman named Bonnie. She was part of the management team, and interestingly, her background was in finance. There were six plants in the USA, so it is commendable the company found a woman capable of running one of them.

Everyone, males and female, feared Bonnie. She was known to be super-aggressive, and everyone was afraid to speak to her. She was rarely seen having lunch with anyone, and I heard people say she was a horrible person who did not support other women. The matter-of-fact way that people spoke about Bonnie was disturbing. The hostility should never have been tolerated, let alone accepted. I'm sure she knew how much people disliked her and I'm sure that was difficult from a sense of belonging.

After I had heard all of the negativity about her, I had the opportunity to work with Bonnie on a project. The company engineers were working on a new system to stream line the fun-size chocolate bar (popular for Halloween) manufacturing process. By installing a new chocolate line, we were able to shift production between the Canada, Waco, and Chicago plants, spreading capacity. This simple change made a big difference in the chocolate bar profitability due to a more efficient utilization of capacity.

I worked with Bonnie to make the production changes, which included redeployment of equipment and materials. She was a pleasure to work with. She was smart, exacting, and even friendly and supportive. She knew what she was doing, and it became clear that she could run circles around most of the other plant managers. In reflection, Bonnie was just fighting for her position, and she was probably lonely. I think she got a bad rap.

The question remains, was Bonnie unsupportive to some women? Perhaps but support and respect are a two-way street.

Sometimes there is uncertainty or a lack of support in organizations that adhere to a rigid structure. Roles are unclear, and people experience the stress of not belonging. Also, women like Bonnie may feel threatened by

© The Author(s) 2018
L. Mattia, *Gender on Wall Street*,
https://doi.org/10.1007/978-3-319-75550-2_9

the scarcity of their status. They feel isolated, and instead of identifying with other women, they may resort to unsupportive behavior.

Mentor Insight: We all need to become aware of how we can support each other. We need to work on developing better relationships and understanding. Women don't always naturally band together, which is why you may want to seek out organizations that actively foster empathy and agreement.

Mars was an interesting place. People had stories about everything and everybody. I never heard a positive story about a woman in any area of financial management. There was a story about Kathy, who had made it to a controller position, but who also apparently spent a lot of time crying under her desk because she was that emotionally unstable. There were several stories of various women who "acquired their position through sexual favors." The message was that women were incapable of getting promoted on their own merit. I am sure things were said about me, but I remained focused on my goals and didn't allow the gender-specific challenge to distract me.

RESISTANCE TO FEMALES IN SENIOR POSITIONS

An experiment conducted at New York University showed that subordinate females penalize senior females by classifying them as unlikeable or interpersonally hostile.[1] In the experiment, a company letter was read aloud to introduce a newly appointed vice president, along with the specifications of his or her position. The participants of the study were then asked for their reaction to this new vice president based on the information from the letter. The results showed that women characterized higher successful females as unlikeable and hostile.

The research results are an example of female coworkers and subordinates reacting negatively to women who are seen to violate gender stereotypes. The negative penalizations were correlated with the women's self-confidence. The more confident the woman in her own ability to succeed, the less negative she was toward these powerful women. Regardless of where the disconnect lies with women supporting women, the result is a breakdown in the female network.

A similar and earlier in-class experiement done by Frank Flynn and Cameron Anderson (2006) at the New York University Business School, asked students to appraise the resume of an entrepreneur named Howard Roizen. His resume showed that Mr. Roizan had worked at Apple, launched his own software company, and been a partner at a venture capital firm. He was a proficient networker and had very powerful friends including Bill Gates. Colleagues described him as a "catalyst" and a "captain of industry." The

[1] Parks-Stamm, E. J., Heilman, M. E., & Hearns, K. A. (2008). Motivated to penalize: Women's strategic rejection of successful women. *Personality and Social Psychology Bulletin, 34*(2), 237–247.

students thought he'd be an excellent person to have within a company because he was someone who got things done and was likeable.

The interesting part of this experiment was that Mr. Howard Roizen doesn't exist. When students were asked to review the true owner of the resume, Ms. "Heidi" Roizen, they judged her to be more selfish and less desirable than Mr. Howard, even though she was viewed as being equally as effective.[2]

Mentor Insight: The only way we can get other people to change is to change our own behavior. A rising tide floats all boats. There is an opportunity for women to increase their awareness about the frailty of the female network and to commit to making an effort to strengthen it. The power that results could be substantially influential.

Resistance to female leadership in other related fields can provide further insights. Historically, the nurse–doctor relationship is one where the female nurse is acquiescent to the dominant male doctor. Several studies have examined what happens to the nurse–doctor relationship when women are in both roles. The results showed that the doctor's gender influences the relationship. One study found that female doctors received less respect and even less help from nurses than their male colleagues. Female doctors will actively try to reduce status differences between themselves and female nurses to encourage a more supportive work environment. The study further found that, in order to protect the relationship, the female physicians resorted to doing as much work as possible themselves. In some cases, they went so far as to befriend the nurses.[3]

Another study in the medical arena found that 177 female nurse respondents were more willing to serve and defer to male doctors. They perceived female physicians as equal in status, and yet they perceived male physicians to be on an elevated status. The respondents also indicated that they felt the female doctors were more hostile toward them.[4] Perhaps, the lack of respect the nurses showed toward the female doctors created this friction. This study shows the source of conflict to be confounding.

Dr. Pat Heim, a gender expert and CEO of the Heim group, specializes in male and female culture in the workplace. She has found that female coworkers and subordinates often react negatively to women who violate gender stereotypes because women expect to share power.[5] She attributes this expectation to the way women interact as collaborators and integrators. It has

[2] Babcock, L. (2007). Dinner parties and poker games: Setting the table, shaping the game and other negotiation metaphors. *Negotiation Journal, 21*(1), 75–83.

[3] Gjerberg, E., & Kjølsrød, L. (2001). The doctor–nurse relationship: How easy is it to be a female doctor co-operating with a female nurse? *Social Science & Medicine, 52*(2), 189–202.

[4] Zelek, B., & Phillips, S. P. (2003). Gender and power: Nurses and doctors in Canada. *International Journal for Equity in Health, 2*(1), 1.

[5] Heim, P. (1990). Keeping the power dead even. *Journal of American Medical Women's Association, 45*, 232–243.

been shown that women prefer this type of work style to a hierarchical style.[6] According to Dr. Heim and her colleagues, women expect to share ideas, listen to each other, and work collaboratively. A woman who dares to acquire a powerful position is obviously defiant of this expection.

Women tend to have more "friends" at work and they take work personally, which does not always work given certain organizational structures. However, confusion of roles between a boss and a friend can cause resentment. When women exchange intimacy with other women, awkwardness ensues if she then needs to ask her to do something. Some women want to be liked, but inconsistencies in behavior create resentment and distrust.

Another theory is that women have such a strong sense of gender norms and acceptable behaviors that women who do not display adequate levels of humility threaten these beliefs. The incongruence between beliefs and behavior creates a situation which is uncomfortable and unappealing.

If women are uncomfortable with other women in senior positions, they may be less inspired, less supportive, and less engaged. Law professor, Felice Batlan, surveyed 142 legal secretaries to see how they viewed themselves and the role they played in their large law firms. He found that not a single one of them preferred to work for a female partner.[7] There is still another alternative explanation for why women may be less supportive of female leadership. If you consider that most people including secretaries are interested in their own success, the preference to work for males could be related to the fact that the secretaries know men hold the power. Concerned about their own success, they line up behind the person who has the greater probability of success.

According to a 2013 Gallup survey of 2059 adults, women have stronger preferences than men regarding the gender of their boss: 40% of women prefer to work for men (versus 29% of men prefer to work for a man), and 27% of women prefer to work for a woman (versus 18% of men who prefer to work for a woman).[8] The good news is that in instances where individuals actually worked for a female boss, the percentage of both males and females who prefer to work for a woman increases, which indicates they had a positive experience.

I met a woman named Fran who held a senior position and came to one of our Women's Advocacy Circle programs. She expressed concern that women did not support each other. Her goal for attending the program was to help change that. Fran had been working as a financial planner at a small

---

[6] Kingsbury, K. B. (2013). *How to give financial advice to couples: Essential skills for balancing high-net-worth clients' needs.* McGraw Hill Professional.

[7] Batlan, F. (2010). "If you become his second wife, you are a fool": Shifting paradigms of the roles, perceptions, and working conditions of legal secretaries in large law firms. In *Special issue law firms, legal culture, and legal practice* (pp. 169–210). Emerald Group Publishing Limited.

[8] http://www.gallup.com/poll/165791/americans-prefer-male-boss.aspx.

independent wealth management firm. She was one of five advisors (the only one with a CFP®) and the only female advisor. She liked her job and was very successful in building client relationships. She created many of the client communication tools used at the firm; designing face-to-face presentations and on-line webinars to educate clients and prospects. Eventually, she became the face of the firm. She felt proud that her contributions had significantly grown the business.

Her fellow (male) advisors were happy she was attracting business to the firm, but Fran began to notice the three women in support staff roles were not very accommodating. They had all chosen traditional roles consistent with gender norms, working as administrators and para planners. All three women were very bright and could have done whatever they wanted if they chose to. Fran saw there was a clear difference between how the women treated her and how they treated the male advisors. As she told me the story, she admitted that they seemed to see her as a woman first, not as one of the professionals. Fran's authority and contributions were not revered on the same level as the men.

As time went on, the lack of cooperation from the support staff became more and more frustrating. The male advisors could simply say, "I need this report" without even a please, but Fran would say, "I know you are busy. I am meeting with a client tomorrow morning; could you possibly help me?" She began to feel like she had to beg and plead for support. There were other reasons why Fran eventually left the firm but the lack of cooperation was a driving force.

Regardless of the cause, if you are stuck in a situation where people are sabotaging your work and are uncooperative, you should distance yourself from the situation. Fran lamented that the real shame was that she left due to the hostile environment created by the females at the office, not the males, which was not what she would have expected.

Mentor Insight: It is difficult to send consistent messages all of the time but this is particularly important with women who work for you. Since the relationship has the potential of feeling uncomfortable or unnatural, a good way to negate those feelings is to always be consistent and fair. It will go a long way toward building subordinate's confidence and trust.

Not All Women Are Committed to the Cause

Cathy is a CFA® who decided to leave her firm for a promotion at a new firm. At first, she was excited to find out her new boss was a woman but then she wasn't so sure. Candice was 49 and had been working at the firm since she first got out of college. She started as a secretary and worked her way up, passing all three of the CFA® modules. She was annoyed, however, because she was given a management position running a passive indexed fund, while younger male colleagues who had not proven themselves were running the actively managed funds. Of course, Cathy was put in Candice's group.

Soon after she started the position, Cathy completed her first trimester of pregnancy. She decided she should tell her boss that she was pregnant since she wanted to be fully upfront. She had only been with the firm for five months and was horrified at Candice's response. "Why didn't you tell us you were pregnant when we interviewed you? If you weren't pregnant then, you should have told us you were trying! No one is going to take you seriously, and you are going to make me look bad."

Sure enough, Candice was right. In fact, she led the pack in terms of not taking Cathy seriously. When an attractive project became available, perfectly matching Cathy's skill set, Candice refused to recommend her for the position. Cathy was disheartened. She had every intention of returning back to work after she delivered her baby, but didn't because she felt that she had been dismissed by the only other woman at the firm. After being away from work for three years, she now feels she's been gone so long it would not be worth it to go back.

Hostile and Benevolent Sexism

Peter Glick from Lawrence University and Susan Fiske from the University of Massachusetts at Amherst developed a theoretical framework around ambivalent sexism which is composed of two types of prejudices against women: hostile and benevolent sexism. Although many people see benevolent sexism as harmless, it can be damaging to women and gender equality, but it works in a different way than hostile sexism.

Glick and Fiske found that women who adhere to gender norms will stereotype other women and themselves in a benevolent way with no mal intent.[9] On the surface, benevolent sexism seems benign, but it can hinder a woman's confidence due to its limitations.

Another study done by Mabel Abraham shows that any kind of sexism is harmful to the success of women regardless of intent. The study looked at senior women in financial services organizations to see if these women used their positions of power to reduce gender inequalities within their organization. She looked at all of the employees in 120 retail branches of the firm: 75% of the staff were women, and 44% of the branch managers were women.

Abraham directly measured the impact of male versus female managers on the career outcomes of their employees. She found that even when women had the ability to promote other women and pay them equally, the female managers did not help their female subordinates get ahead or earn more.

[9]Glick, P., & Fiske, S. T. (2011). Ambivalent sexism revisited. *Psychology of Women Quarterly, 35*(3), 530–535.

Various scholars posit the reason for this is that women fear their reputations will be adversely impacted if they promote and advocate for women who are perceived to be less capable than the men. They feel they risk being negatively judged by others in the organization.[10]

Mentor Insight: Successful women in finance have sacrificed and invested to prove themselves, win trust and be perceived as a valuable contributor so they may be reluctant to take the risk of promoting a woman if there is any doubt. The stereotype supports men as being more capable than women, so they are considered less of a risk. This is a form of sexism, but it is not done out of malice, so it is not considered harmful yet the results are the same—it is a gender-specific challenge to female success.

Recently at the FPA national conference in Nashville, a young lady approached the panel of women in a session called Women at the Forefront of Financial Planning. She asked why senior women are downright unsupportive of younger women. The three millennial women behind me began to whisper, "that's right, good question." I was disappointed in the initial response from the panel when one woman protested, oh no, not possible. But Nicole Perkins, a black woman who had just finished discussing oppression and discrimination associated with the intersectionality of being both black and a woman, said the most courageous and profound commentary I have heard in a very long time. In her desire to be authentic, she admitted that she recently looked around the table at the leadership team she developed with another diverse member and thought, oh no, are there too many of us now? What are people going to think? Should I not recruit any more to join since their presence could reduce our credibility? She admitted, even though she was the victim of unconscious bias, that she too was affected by this unconscious bias lens. Stop Everything. Yes, I too have had a similar experience. What a commentary! I spoke to Nicole after and we both lamented this truth—we have a lot of work to do as a society and as women before we escape the ever present grasp of unconscious bias. It all starts by being honest.

FEMALE BULLIES

There is another gender-specific challenge where women harm women. It has been shown that although men bully other men more than they bully women in the workplace, when women bully, 68% of the time they bully other women.[11] Bullying behavior includes verbal abuse, humiliation, threats and intimidation, and reoccurring and frequent work interference. This is a

---

[10]Abraham, M. L. B. (2013). *Does having women in positions of power reduce gender inequality in organizations?: A direct test* (Doctoral dissertation, Massachusetts Institute of Technology).

[11]http://www.workplacebullying.org/2014-gender/.

topic that makes many of us uncomfortable, but many studies have shown women mistreating other women.[12] Maybe this is just a continuation of high school where girls learn to be critical of each other as they compete for boys' attention, or perhaps, some women have become so aggressive, they cannot control themselves. Maybe women bullies enjoy the power and pick on what they perceive to be the weaker gender. One thing we do know from all of the research is that women are struggling to figure out how to behave and be successful in the workplace, and there are not enough role models to refer to.

Mentor Insight: When working with unsupportive women remember—none of this is personal. Stay outside of the sphere of influence of people who are not women's advocates.

One laboratory study showed that some female managers are negative role models and even deter other women from trying to be successful.[13] In this study, middle managers viewed the few senior women as unsuccessful because of the sacrifices they had to make in an unfriendly cultural environment. Rather than motivating the middle managers to aspire to higher-level positions, their observations negatively impacted their aspirations at the firm.

There are many stories of women who felt a woman in a senior position actively humiliated them, much like my experience with Dana at Mars. Clinical psychologist, Dr. Ruth Namie, had a personal encounter with a boss named Sheila. She describes Sheila as the "boss from hell" whose irrational behavior turned Dr. Namie's career and personal life upside down.[14]

Because a woman was harassing her and not a man, she was told by HR the behavior was not illegal or worthy of consideration. Same gender targets cannot file a claim of discrimination. Due to discrimination laws that are focused on sexual harassment or coercion, 80% of same sex bulling incidents do not lend themselves to a legal complaint. But bullying is not about sex; it is about power and discouraging and dispiriting someone from pursuing a successful career. Since it is difficult to get HR (or anyone else) to help due to the inadequacy of the law, we need to use our emotional and personal power to effect change. Dr. Namie's story reminded me of my Dana experience. The HR manager told me the same thing and said not to rock the boat since I would be perceived as the problem. There were no laws to protect against harassment and intimidating behavior if it came from someone of the same sex.

Dr. Namie and her husband, Dr. Gary Namie, a social psychologist, founded the Workplace Bullying Institute in California after they learned there is an international movement against workplace bullying in countries such as Australia, South Africa, Canada, and New Zealand. In Sweden, for

[12]http://www.tony-silva.com/eslefl/miscstudent/downloadpagearticles/womenagainstwomen-nyt.pdf.

[13]Cross, C., linehan, M., & Murphy, C. (2017). The unintended consequences of role modeling behavior in female career progression. *Personnel Review, 46*(1).

[14]http://www.workplacebullying.org/history-of-wbi/.

example, the phenomenon is called "mobbing." The USA had no such program and the Namies stepped into fill the gap.

Mentor Insight: When bullied by a woman, there is no legal protection because it is not considered "sexual harassment" although it actually could be sexual. Still this misses the point. Harassment is about power, putting someone in their place and discouraging aspirations of success. Hopefully most HR departments are more prepared to deal with this situation but if you require outside assistance contact the Workplace Bullying Institute in California at http://www.work-placebullying.org.

Women may sabotage each other in fear of losing their own careers. They seem to have the thought that there isn't room for more than one token woman. I remember reading an article where the author discussed the idea of rope ladders. Women climb to senior positions and roll up the ladder right behind them. While some women tactically avoid helping other women in their careers, others resort to passive-aggressive behavior to protect their interests.

FINDING COMMON GROUND

Bad relationships at work are toxic. You may not be responsible for the toxicity, but you may be able to use your personal power to fix it. Cindy, a senior financial advisor, recounted an experience with a woman in her office, Julia, who was in her 50s and part of the management team.

Cindy saw Julie in the cafeteria and asked her why she hadn't RSVP'd to a coworker's baby shower. Julia was brutally direct. She said she couldn't believe that Susan got pregnant just when she was recently received a promotion to senior advisor. She said:

> "These younger women act so entitled. All of you younger women are like that. When I was starting out, I didn't expect to be taken seriously if I took the time away from work to have a baby. When I did get pregnant, I worked until the day I delivered. Then, I came back to work two weeks later as if I had just taken a short vacation. I was proud that people hardly noticed I'd had a baby. The worst part of this is that I am going to have to take care of Susan's clients while she is gone. I had to work very hard to get where I am and now Susan is reinforcing the stereotype that women need to be treated differently." She turned to Cindy and asked, "Don't you understand life is about hard choices?"

Senior, often older women, feel that a committed individual must commit to work 24×7 to be successful. This was an important lesson for me and others like me. We need to check ourselves. Although we were willing to work 60–70 hours and put up with onerous job requirements to be successful, that doesn't make it right and it doesn't mean that we should perpetuate this environment.

Mentor Insight: As a senior woman or someone who has found their footing, be aware and empathetic toward women who are still struggling to learn how to behave in the financial services culture. Be a role model for other women. Establish mentorship as part of the culture within your organization.

At first, Cindy was really offended but she then realized Julia had been through a difficult time. Instead of taking a negative stance and declaring war, she decided to see if they could find common ground. She spent more time in the lunchroom talking to Julia about her career and what she had learned over the years. As she spent more time with Julia, not only did Cindy gain a greater respect for her and what she had accomplished, she was also able to explain to Julia why things need to change. She explained that the old, gender biased way is not healthy for the firms, the financial advisors, or the clients. They even agreed philosophically that financial advisors who share their lives with their clients can build more authentic relationships with clients.

Mentor Insight: As women, we need to know how to negotiate our relationships. If done right, both parties can win. The power issue can be resolved by finding common ground and establishing mutual respect. If you're new in your career and a senior woman is unsupportive, help her see the opportunity to support you. Try asking for help. The women advocacy circles discussed in Chapter 12 may inspire you.

Regardless of whether you get help from other women, you need to be focused on your goals to create success. When you stop to set goals you proactively take over your career as opposed to letting others who don't have your best interest in mind influence your career. Goals give you focus away from the gender-specific challenges that have the potential to distract you and undermine your performance. Your personal goals can motivate and inspire you more than a mentor or any other external source.

Exercise: Developing S.M.A.R.T Goals

Developing goals is the first step in claiming your financial career. Goals are dynamic and forever changing. At least once a year, goals need to be reviewed and established for the upcoming year. Goals should be shared with your boss and others who are invested in your success. Establish an evaluation period so your team knows what you are trying to achieve, why and what assistance is needed from others.

Create S.M.A.R.T. goals that support you, your boss, and the firm. A S.M.A.R.T. goal is defined as one that is specific, measurable, achievable, results-focused, and time-bound. Below is a definition of each of the S.M.A.R.T. goal criteria.

Specific: Goals should be clearly defined in terms of what you are going to do. Being specific is the What, Why, and How of the S.M.A.R.T. model.

Example: By August 11, implement new retirement distribution model (what) so that it adequately captures decisions made around taxes, various social security strategies, and the cost of Medicare (why) by working with the IT team and para planners (how).

Measurable: Goals should be measurable so you have tangible evidence that you have accomplished the goal. In addition to achieving the goal, there may be some short-term or smaller measurements built into the goal.

Example: By August 11, implement new retirement distribution model. (The measurement of this goal is dependent upon whether there is a useable new retirement distribution model.)

Achievable: Goals should be achievable and well defined. You must possess the appropriate knowledge, skills, and abilities to achieve the goal. You can meet almost any goal when the steps are planned wisely and a timeframe has been established.

Example: In order for you to reach this goal, you must have a skill set, in this case in the area of financial planning, that allows you to understand the nature of the goal, and the goal must present a large enough benefit to the firm and the work that you do to inspire you in accomplishing it.

Results-focused: Goals should measure outcomes, not activities.

Example: The result of this goal is the new retirement distribution model (Developing this model allows you and your boss to evaluate your performance and develop your career).

Time-bound: Goals should be linked to a timeframe. A deadline creates a sense of urgency and results in tension between the current reality and the vision of the goal. Without such tension, the goal is unlikely to be achieved.

Example: August 11, 20XX

S.M.A.R.T. Goal Questionnaire

This questionnaire will assist you in creating S.M.A.R.T. goals.

Begin by writing your goal as clearly and concisely as possible. Then, answer the related questions. Consider the prior exercises in the preceding chapters as you contemplate your goals. Have you identified changes that need to occur to develop and communicate your brand?

Make copies of this worksheet and refer back to it frequently to track progress. Develop 3–5 goals using the following structure;

Goal:

1. Specific. Why is this goal important? What will the goal accomplish? How and why will it be accomplished?

_____
_____
_____
_____
_____

2. Measurable. Is this goal motivational? How will you measure whether or not the goal has been reached? (List at least two indicators)

_____
_____
_____
_____
_____

3. Achievable. Is the goal obtainable or is it completely unrealistic? Have others done it successfully? Do you have the necessary knowledge, skills, abilities, and resources to accomplish the goal? Will meeting the goal challenge you?

_____
_____
_____
_____
_____

4. Results-focused. What is the reason, purpose, or benefit of accomplishing the goal? What is the outcome of the goal?

_____
_____
_____

_____

_____

5. Time-bound. Is this goal trackable? What is the established completion
   date?

_____

_____

_____

_____

_____

PART III

The STAR Plan

CHAPTER 10

Strategic Framework—Build Your Brand

I was flying home from Madrid to Newark on British Air in the summer of 2000. I had just spent a week reviewing the financial books, records, and projections of Telefónica, S.A. a Spanish multinational broadband and telecommunications provider. I was writing up some notes as I was formulating my opinion on whether Telcordia Technologies should acquire the company.

In sum, my recommendation was not to buy the company due to a lack of synergy relative to the markets and culture of the two companies. Evaluating the purchase relative to the Telcordia's strategic plan/priorities made the answer crystal clear. The strategic plan had been developed by incorporating the organization's: (1) vision/values; (2) strengths, weakness, opportunities, and threats; (3) the stakeholders involved; and (4) goals.

What made Telefónica attractive was its technological expertise but we were already strong in that department: Telcordia had some of the smartest minds in the world. Our weakness was our cost structure. We needed to find cost-cutting opportunities to improve profitability and efficiency. The potential acquisition would make our weakness worse, particularly at the price they wanted. Evaluating the decision relative to the strategic plan made the decision crystal clear. The purchase didn't make sense.

I was sitting in business class with a glass of wine, pouring over the numbers just one more time on the flight. Although I usually keep to myself when flying, the gentleman next to me started a conversation, and I engaged in the discussion. He asked me a lot of questions: What did I do professionally? How did I get into finance? These were not unusual questions, but then he said, "Clearly, you have an important job. You obviously make good money and get to travel internationally. You must love your job!"

His observation made me pause. Do I *love* my job? What kind of question was that? Well yeah, I guess. I don't know. I always thought I was going to help people—transform lives. I wanted to make a difference. I was recording and reporting what other people did. Not only was I not helping

© The Author(s) 2018
L. Mattia, *Gender on Wall Street*,
https://doi.org/10.1007/978-3-319-75550-2_10

people, I wasn't part of making things happen either. The engineers and scientists at my company—they made things happen; they invented and created. That's what was exciting. Perhaps it was the red wine. (My husband always told me red wine was like a truth serum for me.) Or, maybe I was just stressed by the prospect of delivering bad news to the Telcordia management team. Why was I telling a random stranger on a plane all of this information?

It wasn't the first time I had thought about whether I was really satisfied and happy with my job. However, it was the first time I vocalized it and the verdict was, no, I didn't love (or even like) my job. I just did it. Wow! life is too short to coast on autopilot. I knew I needed to do something, and the first place to start was with a plan.

THE STAR PLANNING PROCESS:
CREATE A STRATEGIC CAREER PLAN

As a senior finance executive, I have been involved in developing many plans: operating plans, capital budgeting plans, marketing plans, business plans, product plans, and strategic plans. What I needed was a strategic plan for my career; a strategic plan that could drive my career decision making and render the answers crystal clear.

I decided to start by collecting data about myself. The process was similar to what I did for corporations but also similar to what we do for clients when creating a financial plan. The main components of any plan involve having a vision for where you want to end up, recognizing where you are now, and then identifying the necessary steps to bridge the gap. Financial planners focus on client goals and compare them to the client's current situation using financial statements, such as the net worth and cash flow statements. They identify the gap and explore options to bridge the gap to help the client reach their goals. This decision-making process is the same conceptually in every planning opportunity.

I used a corporate approach for my strategic career plan. The only difference was I *started* with my desired outcomes by concentrating on my vision and an amalgamation of my values. A vision is a higher order than goals since it defines your purpose. It can send you on a different trajectory than if you focus only on goals.

The vision is the right place to start. It should define what you stand for. Think of it in terms of what you want to be remembered for—your legacy. What do you want written on your epitaph? I know it sounds creepy, but you get the drift. For clients who let me, this is where I begin our financial planning conversation, not with goals. When you start with your life's purpose, your vision, and values, it opens up possibilities and avenues that may not be considered if you go directly to a conversation about goals. This chapter is about focusing on possibilities and the very essence of *you*. Why are you on this planet and how do you want your career to affect your legacy.

Creating a strategic career plan is a form of conscious engagement which activates your time, energy, and resources to support your values. If you google the term "conscious engagement," you won't find it. It is a term I use after thirty years of "planning," coaching individuals, managing financial teams, and even group facilitation work done while studying psychology. I'm sure life and career coaches use similar techniques, because it works. While the process is excellent for developing a comprehensive personal plan for all aspects of your life (and I highly advise you use it that way), this book concentrates on developing your career.

The process is motivated by your desired career outcomes and results (your vision/values) while understanding your current situation (your strengths, weaknesses, opportunities, and threats) and managing your relationships (particularly with your key stakeholders), while prioritizing and focusing on daily activities (aligned with your goals). It is a disciplined effort that produces decisions to guide what you do, who you serve, and why do you do it.

Effective strategic career planning articulates not only where you are going and the actions needed to make progress, but also how you will evaluate your progress and success. This type of planning should feel comfortable to the financial planner since the process is similar to financial planning, which should be approached in a thoughtful and serious manner.

Identify Your Values

The STAR process revolves around your values. Figure 10.1 illustrates the different aspects of your strategic career plan starting with your values and proceeding through each area, as they affect revisions to your goals.

The key objective is to find a career consistent with your values. For example, one of my key personal career values linked to my vision is *transforming lives* (in the values exercise this would fall under influencing lives). I am energized by the possibility of helping people change the trajectory of their life and helping them achieve happiness. I am very interested in personal *responsibility* and taking full control over one's life. I want to know the *truth*, not what I want the truth to be, but the reality. I believe the only way you can implement change is by first understanding the exact truth. These values are all important to me.

As I developed my set of values, an interesting truth about myself was revealed. Although I selected *security* as an important value, I realize that I am not concerned about having money. For me, security is about having marketable skills so I can always find interesting work. This explains my excessive pursuit of secondary education. Certainly, if I was primarily motivated by money, I could have stayed in the corporate sector and taken on new roles to increase my income while ignoring my bigger purpose.

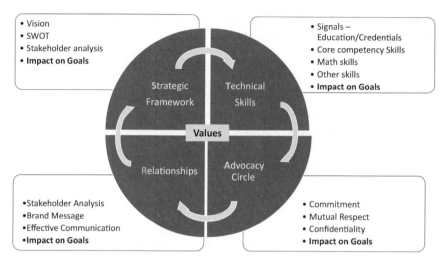

Fig. 10.1 The STAR plan: your strategic career plan

This personal observation highlights the importance of understanding what each value actually means to you; security means different things to different people. As a result of exploring my values, I've also learned that I am motivated by non-pecuniary compensation in the form of *respect, acknowledgment, and appreciation* for my efforts and competence.

Knowing this about myself has been invaluable. Now, I know why I was not satisfied in certain jobs or working with certain people. I know why I didn't like working with "master of the universe" types who wanted to be the only one in charge and intimidated by my success and recognition. I know why working in roles where I was reporting and recording information did not satisfy my need to touch people personally. I also know why working with individuals in denial of reality, who were unable to acknowledge obvious problems, made me crazy. That type of behavior flew in the face of dealing with truth and being responsible. Really understanding your values helps you identify environments where you will be successful. Values are the building blocks for your vision and the rest of your strategic career plan.

When I first did the exercise of listing my values and then listing what I did in my job, nothing lined up. No wonder I wasn't satisfied. In the process of working through your values in the Chapter 2 exercise, you have already begun to define your passion and what is important to you. As you start iterating your plan, you will naturally go back and refine your work values, perhaps several times. This is a period of discovery where you take the time to sort out who you are.

The process can be very uncomfortable for some women, especially those who have allowed other people to persuade them to do what they thought was best. For the women who were "good girls" and let their fathers or other authoritative figures dictate what you should do, this is the time for you to take charge of your career and your life.

Develop Your Vision

I play golf. I would not call myself a golfer since I'm not very good but I have been playing for almost twenty-five years. One of the first things you learn in golf, after all of the etiquette, is that you need to keep your eye on the ball. As you set up the ball, swing the club back, and make contact with the ball, your eyes need to be focused on the ball the entire time. Most golfers will tell you that, although your eyes are on the ball, your thoughts are on the target, which is where you want the ball to land.

Top players know they need "to vision" where the ball will go. This is trickier than one might expect. When I get to a water hole, even if the water is off to the side, I take out a ball that I don't mind loosing. This is because I tend to inadvertently make the water my target. Even though I would like my vision to be the hole by the flag, I allow my mind to get distracted by the challenge instead of the positive outcome. So, if my mind is focused on the water, guess where my ball goes—of course, the water!

Mentor Insight: The clearer and more single-minded your vision, the fewer obstacles will divert your performance. For this reason, your vision is not only your aspiration; it is also your defense.

Following that pivotal British Air flight, I decided to put pen to paper and began writing about what I wanted for my life, my vision. I wrote for an hour about everything that came to mind, even why I thought I was born. (I know I may lose some of you at this point.) It might sound a little arrogant to think I was born for a purpose or that I can accomplish things beyond most people's wildest dreams. But why not me? And why not you? If you don't plan out your vision for your life, then life will just happen and you will get whatever it gives you. I know this to be fact. People who don't vision get stuck in a hopeless cycle of passing time in life without aspiration or joy but every single successful person I know has a vision for their life.

For example, perhaps your vision is to become very wealthy and start a foundation to financially support female entrepreneurs. Your vision might be to acquire fame and become the next Suzie Orman. You might have a vision like mine and aspire to transform lives by helping people change the trajectory of their success. If I were to articulate my vision further it would be similar to my top value of influencing people. My ultimate vision for my life is that, "The world and people I meet are better off because of my wisdom, compassion, and love. I make a positive difference in the world."

Your life's vision is the big picture which defines who you want to be, what you want to be known for, and the set of outcomes and accomplishments you aim for. It helps define your goals by giving you a framework. Your vision is your why, not your how. It represents what you want your brand to stand for in the eyes of your stakeholders and clients. The articulation of your vision can work like magic for brand building and messaging.

It also needs to inspire and motivate you. It will define your principles, and your sense of right and wrong. It is a mind-set that calibrates and guides how you approach your job. It is optimistic and provides a benchmark for you to measure every goal and activity you take on.

The interchange between vision and values can be a little confusing. Your vision could be a direct expression of an important value or it can be an amalgamation of a group of values. I start with my values, create a single overarching vision for my career, and then also articulate the vision for each of my values. (I'll show you an example of my process in the upcoming redefining goals section.) As you work on your goals, hold them up against your vision to ensure they are aligned with your higher purpose. Define your vision (your reason for being/your purpose) so it is powerful enough to keep you going even during the times when everything goes wrong (those days, weeks, and months happen for all of us). Your vision will inspire you to jump out of your bed every morning and try again.

Refine Your Goals

Once you have clarified your vision and values, revisit your goals. Do they align with your values? Do they capitalize on your strengths and take advantage of opportunities? Do they protect you from the weaknesses that could make you vulnerable to possible threats? Do they address what you need to do to develop relationships with your stakeholders? (Maybe not completely.) The process must be an iterative one, where you go back and revisit your goals frequently. They should and will change as you become clearer in what you need to do to assure your success. Goals aligned with vision and purpose are a winning strategy, especially when you've taking into account your own characteristics and the people around you.

When I was getting my MBA, a fellow student named Sheila and I often studied together. She used a Franklin Planner to schedule our meetings and organize her thoughts. She convinced me to try using the time management system, and I was immediately hooked. It encouraged me to plan my day in a way that was consistent with my goals.

The Franklin Planner was my first official strategic planning tool, and I still carry it with me every day. In these days of electronics, people look at me a little funny but there's something about writing things down that appeals to me. I've heard that the act of writing something down is more committal than keying it into an electronic device. Although I have not looked into the research, I believe it's the case for me.

The other tool that I have used for planning is Excel. After I wrote my vision, I created an Excel spreadsheet that captured each of my values and how they supported my vision. From there, I created goals to incorporate the values into my vision. I know, not everyone is hooked on Excel so it doesn't have to be so systemized. However you go about it, the point is to capture how your vision will manifest itself in the different important areas of your life.

My values are the strategic pillars that I focus on. The following are two examples of how I have expanded on my values, describing the specific vision relative to the value and one S.M.A.R.T. goal that I will work on to achieve the vision and live out that value. The first value is indirectly related to my career. Because it is important to me, it is part of my "comprehensive" strategic career plan.

FAMILY: *Allowing Time for Family*

Vision: My family values honesty. We support and encourage each other to achieve our life goals through respect, love, kindness, and patience. We seek to resolve conflict and celebrate life.

One S.M.A.R.T. goal to support this vision: Have family dinner at least 4 times a week where we all spend time together without cell phones, in a pleasant environment.

- Specific: "Have dinner together, without cell-phones in a pleasant environment" is important because it gives everyone time to connect with each other and remind each other how important we are to each other.
- Measurable: "4 times a week" is motivational since these family dinners become the highlight of my and my husband's day. Despite a couple of missed parties, I think my children enjoy them too.
- Achievable: This is defined well enough that it is achievable and even if I have work commitments several times a week, I can adjust what I am doing over the weekend to achieve the goal.
- Results-focused: The outcome is having a pleasant dinner; there is no detail on where or how. If there is no time for meal preparation, we go out to dinner. If it is late at night, we make sandwiches and sit at the table on the lanai by the fireplace. The focus of the activity is pleasant communal shared family time.
- Time-Bound: Since the activity is every week, it is trackable.

INFLUENCING PEOPLE: Influencing Opinions and Behaviors of Women

Vision: Encourage women to become engaged in household, corporate, and world finances for the greater good by empowering women in financial services to become leaders.

One S.M.A.R.T. goal to support this vision: Encourage ten young women per year to enroll in a CFP Board-certified financial planning degree program and provide them with tools to help them be successful.

- Specific: "Encouraging women to commit to a degree in personal financial planning" will be a win for the female student, win for the university, win for the industry, and win for society as a whole.
- Measurable: "Ten women per year" is motivational since preparing these young ladies' for success will result in more women entering and *remaining* in the financial services industry.
- Achievable: This is defined well enough that it is achievable since I can do this working as a Program Director of Personal Finance at my current university and through my affiliations as a visiting professor at other universities.
- Results-focused: The outcome is enrolling ten women in a degree program. If I am unable to achieve that at my university, I might influence young women who have read this book or who have heard me speak to enroll at another university.
- Time-Bound: Since the activity is every year, it is trackable. However, there may be women who enroll in a degree program and I am unaware if they were motivated by the work I've done. This is a potential snare in the plan but not enough of an issue to deter the goal. (If you have chosen to pursue a financial services career as a result of my persuasion, please let me know ☺.)

The other values/strategic pillars that I have attached to S.M.A.R.T. Goals are;

- RESPONSIBILITY: Demonstrating trustworthiness and reliability.
- MORAL/SPIRITUAL: Living out ideals or moral code.
- RECOGNITION: Receive positive feedback and acknowledgment of good work.
- ACCOMPLISHMENT: Setting goals and achieving them.
- INTELLECTUAL CHALLENGE: Keeping the mind active and constantly thinking.
- ALTRUISM: Helping and advising others for the greater good.

Every year, I revisit my primary vision and write for an hour to determine my values/strategic pillars. The vision and values don't change much but they have evolved, and I have gained more clarity and color each time I do this exercise. My goals, on the other hand, change regularly, as well as the way I plan to satisfy each value/strategic pillar.

Goals that support my responsibility, accomplishment, and recognition values have changed the most based upon where I am working, my role, and the needs of the organization. I have taken one value off of my list—EDUCATION. My family has tolerated enough homework filled weekends and holidays. INTELLECTUAL CHALLENGE remains but is satisfied through my affiliation with a university and a firm full of highly intelligent and educated people who share their human capital with me every day.

TRANSFORMING LIVES

When I first began the strategic planning process, after the Madrid trip, my initial analysis revealed that my goals were in conflict with my values. I recognized that I could satisfy my key career value—TRANSFORMING LIVES—by applying my financial and educational skills to help people achieve financial success.

I was already providing 401k investment guidance at the company where I worked and had helped several women evaluate their property settlement while pursuing divorce. The women who sought my guidance were looking for someone to trust and counted on me to give them good advice. I spent a lot of time thinking about my recommendations and realized that if I was going to do this professionally I needed more than my MBA in accounting/finance. I decided to pursue the CFP®, which is the top credential in the profession. I also decided that I would work as a fee-only financial advisor because I wanted to serve as a true fiduciary 100% of the time.

I strategically planned out my career change. At the time, I was making a very good salary. My family counted on me, so I couldn't just walk away from it. Instead, I established myself at Geller and Company (a firm I mentioned earlier), which hired me to work in their emerging markets division because of my experience as a CFO. They also hired me for potential future needs as a new CFP® candidate to work in their family office division.

At the same time, I connected with a small fee-only firm where I held an Investment Advisor Representative (IAR) license and began taking on clients to develop the experience credit for the CFP®. To accelerate that credit, I also worked at H&R Block on Saturdays and Sundays. As I worked, I was careful to save funds for my transition because I assumed my income would drop. The process of completing the CFP® requirements and finding the right opportunity to execute my plan took eight years but I was inspired and motivated by my vision.

When the time came for me to make the transition, I ended up with two opportunities. Geller offered me a position in the family office which served ultra high net worth individuals. This was an incredible prospect: great paying, challenging and I would continue to develop my expertise in financial planning. The downside was that I had not developed a real sense of belonging at Geller (as I mentioned earlier). I was also offered a partner position at the fee-only firm, which had a strong need for my particular skill set.

My husband thought I was crazy for considering the fee-only firm, particularly since the starting compensation would be around 15% of the Geller job offer. Still the position satisfied a need of mine in a way the Geller position did not. I could transform lives working with people who really needed guidance. I would also be in a position where my qualifications were especially needed. This satisfied my other important work values such as recognition, respect and appreciation. I took the fee-only position.

When I began working as a full-time fee-only advisor, I got involved in the National Association of Personal Financial Planners (NAPFA) and became the NYC study group leader. In 2008, NAPFA launched a campaign called "Your Money Bus" where we offered pro bono financial advice all over the city. It was an eye-opening experience.

I'll never forget the day (October 15th) I was told to meet a reporter by the NASDAQ building at 5 p.m. to discuss our talking points about spreading financial literacy. I showed up but had not listened to the news since we were up in Harlem all day providing pro bono financial advice. Recession talk had scared Wall Street and the Dow Jones Industrial Average experienced its second biggest one-day point loss ever. Falling 733 points, the decline was second only to the September 29th decline a few weeks earlier, when the House of Representatives rejected the government's $700 billion bank bailout plan. Needless to say, the interview was not about responsible financial advice. It turned into a discussion around market volatility, fear, and whether people should sell everything and hide.

What an opportunity! During times of fear, people look for responsible guidance more than ever. I quickly repositioned our firm as *educational* advisors who offered practical fiduciary advice. The messaging was perfect, and we saved numerous people from really bad financial mistakes. We also helped relieve a few more from "unscrupulous" salespeople who were disguised as advisors.

When I first made my transition, I was adamant that the fee-only model was the best way to go, until I began to meet other competent advisors who did not work in the fee-only space. At the same time, I met some fee-only advisors who had become NAPFA registered before the CFP® and educational requirements had been grandfathered. My mind began to change as I realized that if you don't have the human capital to know what is in the client's best interest, you cannot be a fiduciary regardless of how you get compensated. I also believe that possession of human capital and market forces compel advisors to do what is in the client's best interest.

My career strategy remained the same—to transform lives—but the goals changed. Realizing that education and knowledge are key to giving good advice, I decided to join the academics who are forming the future of the financial services profession. As consumers become more educated and demand fiduciaries, they will also demand financial advisors who have received a degree in financial planning, have passed a strenuous exam (the CFP® or CFA®), and receive ongoing ethical training.

In an effort to transform lives both for consumers and for future financial advisors, I decided to go back to school again; this time for a PhD in Personal Financial Planning at the top school in the country for this degree, Texas Tech University. When I sat down with my advisor at TTU to discuss my program itinerary, he looked at me and said, "You realize you will be over 50 years old when you are done with this." I told him, "I'm going to be over 50 years old with the PhD or without the PhD and that I preferred the former." He was satisfied with that answer and we continued to work on my degree for six years. I was inspired by the degree because I had a vision to transform **many** lives by creating a new breed of competent, ethical financial advisors.

I'm sharing this story to illustrate how my goals kept evolving but always aligned with my vision. I continued to follow the strategic planning process of regularly reviewing my vision/values along with the current opportunities, threats, and people in my career life. I then evaluated my goals to determine if they were still aligned or needed to be changed. It's become a ritual I look forward to in January every year.

Your strategic career plan is just like a financial plan. It's obsolete in no time because things change. If you are at a very dynamic time in your life, you might want to review your plan more often—every six months or even once a quarter. Make this planning process work for you so you remain consciously engaged in building your career.

Yes, I have had many twists and turns in my career but if you understand my vision, my purpose and the difference I want to make in the world you can see that it is consistent and I continue to move forward. My vision guides me and inspires me every day, and I literally can't wait to wake up each morning. That is what an aspirational vision does—it creates a rich and fulfilling career. That is what I hope for you, my reader.

YOUR CURRENT SITUATION

Now that you know where you want to go, you need to reassess where you are today. Your vision and your values will help you define your strategic framework. The SWOT analysis helps you identify your internal characteristics and connect them to the external opportunities and threats that exist in your current environment. The stakeholder analysis tells you who is on the bus with you and who has the power to contribute to your success in achieving your goals.

It is an interesting exercise to review your current situation in line with your vision for your career. How disparate or close are you to achieving your vision? If you are miles away, are you willing to do the work to get there or do you need to change something about your current situation? The answer could influence your goals and the hope is that you will find a way to align yourself around your vision since that is what inspires you.

There are circumstances when people need to go back and revisit their vision, usually because they deemed themselves incapable of achieving it. Personally, I think these people are likely selling themselves short. Any vision is attainable if you commit to working on it. What could be more rewarding than being motivated and inspired to work toward your ideal vision?

The commitment to live out your vision may require some changes. If the universe alters your course, find an alternate route but stay motivated and engaged. You may need to retool and transform weaknesses into strengths, or you may need to reposition yourself in a new work environment with more opportunities and fewer threats. Whatever you decide, you need to be aware that you are making these decisions consciously. The choice is yours, which is what conscious engagement is all about.

Exercise: Your Strategic Career Plan

If you completed the exercises in the preceding chapters, your vision for your career should be becoming clear. It is time to commit to paper. Give yourself somewhere between 30 and 60 minutes to complete the first draft of your vision. While writing a vision, don't be intimidated by its importance. Remember this is a constantly changing document and nothing you write is set in stone. As you write, please keep the following in mind:

1. **Shoot for your biggest idea.**

   You can always tone it down in the future but it is always better to aim high.

2. **Write about what moves you and gets you excited beyond everything else.**

   This is about your passion and what motivates you for greatness. This is what will get you up in the morning on that cold winter day. This is what you live for.

3. **Write from the top of your head without thinking and as quickly as you can.**

   Waiting for the exact right words will get in the way of what you are thinking. You can wordsmith the document later. Don't over think; just write as if it is coming from your inner self—you may even be surprised.

4. **Make it a personal commitment.**

   Write it with passion and write it as if it has already happened. There is no doubt that this is your future since you are 100% committed to seeing it happened.

5. **Make it a working, living document.**

   Your vision for your future will evolve and change over time. You will gain more clarity, and you will be able to add more color as you develop it and work on the related pieces of your strategic career plan. It is an iterative process where each aspect of your plan supports and inspires the others. Still your vision needs to be at the helm, so it should be revised accordingly. Every time you make a change, step back and ask yourself if you are inspired and excited by the vision.
   After you have completed your writing, summarize your vision and how it plays into the other components of your plan.

Vision: What is the big picture, your purpose in life?

_____
_____
_____
_____
_____
_____

Values: What are the values which define your purpose in life?

_____
_____
_____
_____
_____
_____

Strengths: What can you rely on to increase your success most times?

_____
_____
_____
_____
_____
_____

Weaknesses: What can you do to reduce your vulnerability to threats?

_____
_____
_____
_____
_____
_____

Opportunities: (where you currently work)

_____
_____
_____
_____
_____

Threats: (where you currently work)

_____
_____
_____
_____
_____

Key Stakeholders: Who are the top people who can make a difference in your career?

_____

_____

_____

_____

_____

_____

What are the top 5–7 goals that you can focus on to achieve your strategic priorities and realize your vision? You may need to go back to add or revise your S.M.A.R.T. goals.

_____

_____

_____

_____

_____

_____

_____

_____

_____

_____

_____

_____

_____

_____

_____

_____

_____

_____

CHAPTER 11

Technical Skills—Fortify Your Brand

Several years ago, I mentored a woman named Karen. When she called me she had been working at a large brokerage house for over ten years. Karen said that she did okay at work but constantly felt pressured to prove herself. She was frustrated and told me that she often saw new male advisors with less experience and knowledge join the business. They seemed to have more credibility than she did with both management and clients. "What is that all about?" she asked rhetorically.

We talked about unconscious bias, gender norms, and how women are not commonly seen as financial experts. Despite the challenges, I explained what things she could do to increase her confidence and credibility. I told her that having a signal, an identifier that communicates her expertise even before someone meets her, could help solve the problem. She had many excuses why she didn't want to "waste the time" to pursue the signals, and she simply did not think it was worth it.

Months later, when her brokerage firm began offering incentives to advisors to get their Certified Financial Planner (CFP®) designation, Karen decided to sign up for a certification program to prepare to take the CFP® examination. She admitted it was time to sharpen her skills and demonstrate what she knew. She completed the program and passed the CFP® examination in her first try. Since she already had the experience working as an advisor, she was able to use the marks immediately. She became listed on the CFP® site and also on the Financial Planning Association (FPA) search engine.

Karen couldn't believe what a difference having the CFP® mark made. She began to get inquiries from new prospects within weeks, but the biggest difference was that she felt she had instant credibility. She no longer had to reiterate the number of years she had been in the business, nor was she questioned about her ethical background. Consumers seemed to understand that a CFP® meant she had studied hard, passed a comprehensive test, taken ethics classes, and was monitored by the CFP Board.

© The Author(s) 2018
L. Mattia, *Gender on Wall Street*,
https://doi.org/10.1007/978-3-319-75550-2_11

Karen also noted that her coworkers seemed to have more respect for her work. In fact, one of the older advisors asked her to partner with him in working with some of his clients since he wanted to transition into preretirement mode. He introduced Karen as the smart new CFP® who complimented his skills. Karen wished she had pursued the certification sooner and agreed that it was a great way for people to filter advisors for quality.

Consumer Conundrum

Financial services offer a valuable service to consumers, keeping them from costly financial decision-making mistakes. It's a smart option for individuals who are not interested or who don't have the time to invest in financial knowledge. However, financial advice is a professional service defined by economists as a "credence good." Even once the consumer experiences the service, they are not fully certain they have received the best quality or outcome. A relationship with a financial advisor requires a leap of faith a lot of people are not willing to take. Consumers are weary about the financial industry, and they don't know who to trust, since anyone can call themselves a financial advisor. So there is a catch 22 where individuals could benefit greatly from professional advice but hesitate to hire someone for fear of making the wrong alliance.

Consumers are also disenchanted with financial services because of agency costs, which are inevitable due to the separation of ownership and control typical of the client/financial advisor relationship.[1] A client, as the principal, delegates some degree of decision making to an advisor (the agent), to provide financial services on his/her behalf. Although both participants have the same notional objective, the separation of ownership and control creates a conflict of interest. Since financial services are a credence good, an information asymmetry exists where the advisor knows more about the quality of their service than the client. Consumers are acutely aware that this information asymmetry has led to advisors working in their own best interest resulting in fraud, abuse, incompetency, and self-serving recommendations that can cost clients billions of dollars.[2]

Although consumers could try to mitigate these losses, most don't have the knowledge or time to evaluate and monitor the advisor's behavior or performance. It is useful to recall what we have learned from behavioral finance theory involving bias and heuristics. Consumers are bombarded with information, and they have limited time and energy to evaluate it all. If only they could receive a signal from above that would tell them who they can trust. Financial service firms often use fancy marketing, meaningless titles and extravagant

[1] Jensen, M. C., & Meckling, W. H. (1976). Theory of the firm: Managerial behavior, agency costs, and ownership structure. *Journal of Financial Economics, 3*(4), 305–360.

[2] Macy, J. (2002). *Regulation of financial planners.* White paper prepared for the FPA.

offices to create signals of competence and ethics, but many savvy consumers recognize these signals as superficial and manipulative. Some people opt to hire an advisor from their church or synagogue since they view that membership as evidence of ethical sentiment.

TRUST AND COMPETENCY SIGNALS

Among the alphabet soup of designations, consumers are confused because they don't know which designations are quality signals. The top internationally recognized gold standard designations are the Certified Financial Planner (CFP®) and the Chartered Financial Analyst (CFA®). Although some overlap exists between these two designations, the skills, expertise, and target markets are different.

Both designations cover a body of knowledge in investment and portfolio management including time value of money and economic concepts, but the CFA® designation focuses primarily on investment and tools for analysis on a deeper level. The CFP® designation is broader, extending into a comprehensive approach that evaluates investments relative to other components of a financial plan. Both designations have a code of ethics and standards of professional conduct. Research involving registered representatives (not fiduciary, Fee-Only, Registered Investment Advisors) has shown that CFP® and CFA® designees are less likely to be cited for misconduct due to the ethical and educational requirements associated with the designations.[3] The requirements to obtain these designations are higher than what the Financial Industry Regulatory Authority (FINRA) requires of registered representatives without these certifications.

As you build your brand, it may be appropriate to choose one designation over the other due to the differences in focus. The CFA® designation is best for investment analysis and portfolio management for high-wealth individual, small business owners, and institutional clients. The CFP® designation is best for a comprehensive approach to assist individuals and families. In actuality, these designations are complimentary, and some advisors obtain both to serve their clients.

No matter how you feel about the CFP® or CFA® education, getting the marks does say that you persevered, committed yourself to achieving the marks, and studied the scientific principals of financial investing/planning. It also says you are committed enough to keep your marks up-to-date with

[3] Camarda, J. (2017). Relationship between Financial Advisory Designations and FINRA Misconduct. This research also includes the ChFC as an ethical designation and is another option for someone who does not want to sit for the CFP® examination. This analysis is robust since advisor misconduct is measurable, monitored, and disclosed to the public by FINRA based on RR U4 disclosures. The analysis was made possible by Eagan et al. (2016) who built a comprehensive database by accessing individual RRs' BrokerCheck records, one at a time, in order to overcome FINRA's reporting limits. They found that 12% of RRs have misconduct disclosures, and 7% have been disciplined for misconduct or fraud who are also five times more likely to be repeat offenders. They also found misconduct more prevalent with elderly and high-income retail clients.

continuing education and to adhere to standards set forth by the CFP Board and the CFA Institute who monitor the ethics of your work. Don't belittle this messaging. It's a powerful signal to a consumer that differentiates you from others who call themselves a financial advisor, portfolio manager, financial planner, or wealth manager.

Those new to the financial advisory field typically pursue education and then take the examination, so they are equipped to land a good job, whether they are new students or career-changers. There are many choices to satisfy the educational requirements ranging from receiving a certificate to getting a degree at the undergraduate or graduate level.

If you are just starting out and do not have a college degree, university programs offering a degree in financial planning, preparing students to sit for the CFP® exam, provide salient signals of academic rigor, motivation, and commitment. These programs provide the intense knowledge required to be in the profession. Students learn to advise in the client's best interest, and the pedagogy often includes fintech, effective communication, sales, behavioral finance, economics, financial statements, business law, critical thinking, and decision-making skills. The student gets immersed in the profession through clubs and professional programs, including internships, competitions, and opportunities to test skills and preferences prior to entering the job market. Most importantly, students who major in financial planning are passionate about the impact they can make on society and in people's lives. University programs are the future of the CFP® profession as they satisify the demand for financial planners in both quantity and quality.

Mentor Insight: The CFP® designation is a signal but it is much more. It exposes you to a comprehensive and broad knowledge based upon scientific principals and insights from a multi-method approach. Even when you are not creating comprehensive or module financial plans, you will find that you are giving financial advice that is not isolated to one topic. The comprehensive curriculum established by the CFP® Board provides the broad knowledge to see the integration of financial decisions which produce optimal recommendations.

When women receive technical training and develop their confidence, they elevate their status to the same level as the men. In fact, some might argue that these women are superior in ability due to strong inherent interpersonal skills. While the window of opportunity for women to enter into financial services continues to widen, women are being given a platform to show their value.

But there will always be doubters. Some people will not believe in your brand. They might think you are overselling your capabilities. That is why your brand must include tangible attributes—most importantly technical knowledge and the evidence and signals of that knowledge. If you skip acquiring the appropriate signals, you may forever be second-guessed. Lack of education or certification communicates a lack of ability or perseverance to acquire what you need.

Technical skills support your brand and most importantly, they support your confidence. I take pleasure in telling the women in the financial planning programs at schools such as Texas Tech University, University of South Florida, Utah Valley University, Akron Ohio, Georgia State, and William Patterson, they are fortunate to have salient skills, and they should wear them as a badge of honor. Everyone in the industry knows the rigor of these programs, and the woman's personal brand is an extension of their university's brand. I tell them to hold their head high and to be confident. Early in your career, your experience is limited and acquiring the right technical knowledge is fundamental to your success.

Harvard University economist Claudia Goldin purports that men often underestimate women's skills based on the fact that there are less women working in finance.[4] Carrying this (mis)logic a step further creates justification for not hiring women since that would lower the productivity and overall success of the firm. Dr. Goldin's research shows that women with salient education and certifications are able to transcend this bias since they have proven that they do have the aptitude. By obtaining the relevant degrees and certifications, you can rise above this discriminating mind-set.

Mentor Insight: Technical knowledge strengthens your brand, your relationships with others, and your confidence. It will empower you to avoid gender obstacles since you are not just your gender—you are a financial expert. Many women are uncomfortable advocating their financial expertise but the right signals do the work for you.

YOUR BRAND AND THE FIDUCIARY STANDARD

Another signal to consumers about the strength of your brand is the business model you choose. It dictates how you are regulated and the standards you are held to. While the financial services industry is heavily regulated, consumers remain apprehensive (and rightfully so). Financial advisors are regulated piecemeal by the various component services they provide leaving plenty of room for a breach of professional conduct. The two primary federal regulations that have existed are delineated based on definitions of investment advisers versus broker-dealers. A third regulator, the Department of Labor (DOL), also has jurisdiction over qualified accounts, which hold deferred compensation for retirement purposes.

The regulatory scheme can get even more complicated with state regulation. To keep this discussion simple, Table 11.1, panel A reviews the primary regulators (along with CFP® Board, which is not a regulator) defining when an advisor is working as a fiduciary.

---

[4] Goldin, C. (2014). A grand gender convergence: Its last chapter. *The American Economic Review, 104*(4), 1091–1119.

Table 11.1 Defining fiduciary (Regulation or Action)

Note: X= Behaving as a Fiduciary REGULATOR:	FINRA	SEC	DOL	Insurance Commission	PRIOR: Two Types of CFP®s		NEW CFP®
					Part Time	Full-Time	Full-Time
REGULATED AS A FIDUCIARY?:	Not Fiduciary	Fiduciary	Fiduciary	Not Fiduciary	Fiduciary	Fiduciary	Fiduciary
Panel A What Regulation Defines Fiduciary?							
Selects Commission Investments for Non-Qualified Funds							X
Selects Commission Investments for Qualified Funds			X				X
Selects fee-only Investments for Non-Qualified Funds		X				X	X
Selects fee-only Investments for Qualified Funds		X	X			X	X
Sells Insurance Product							X
Sells Variable Annuity for Qualified Funds			X				X
Sells Variable Annuity For Non-Qualified Funds							X
Creates a Financial Plan					X	X	X
Panel B What Action Defines Fiduciary?							
Competency							
Basic Education	X	X	X	X	X	X	X
Advanced Education based upon body of knowledge					X	X	X
Experience Requirement					X	X	X
Assessment of Advanced Education - Exam					X	X	X
Trustworthy							
Basic Ethics	X	X	X	X	X	X	X
Ongoing Ethics Education and Commitment					X	X	X
Disclosure of Conflicts		X	X			X	X
Removal of Conflicts		X	X			X	X

Many financial advisors are regulated by the Security and Exchange Committee (SEC) under the Investment Advisers Act of 1940, revised in 1996 to coordinate federal and state regulation. Individuals must register under this act if they pass the three-prong test which includes giving advice or issuing reports about securities, holding one to be in the business of investment advice, and receiving an economic benefit from these services. The Adviser Act includes broad antifraud provisions and entails a fiduciary relationship consisting of three major duties: due care, loyalty, and good faith. These provisions are based on the SEC's belief that investment advisers could not properly do their job unless material conflicts of interest are avoided, or, if conflicts are unavoidable, fully disclosed, consented to by the customer, and fairly managed.

In contrast, the Securities Exchange Act of 1934 (Exchange Act) regulates the secondary distribution of registered securities by brokers who effect transactions, for other people and dealers who buy and sell securities for their own accounts. The SEC and the broker-dealer industry jointly formed what is now called the Financial Industry Regulatory Authority (FINRA) to regulate broker-dealers. Unlike investment advisers, broker-dealers are not required to operate as a fiduciary toward clients. Broker-dealers have no obligation to monitor customer's accounts. The suitability rule governs broker-dealers and requires that recommendations are reasonable and based on the facts the client reveals. FINRA Rules require the broker to "observe high standards of commercial honor and just principals of trade." The language is purposefully vague and allows the self-regulatory organization to determine appropriate enforcement. Brokerage firms now offer fee-based accounts, which has sparked prolonged controversy over regulation and the standard of care given to consumers.

The DOL has historically regulated employer-sponsored accounts under the Employee Retirement Income Security Act of 1974 (ERISA). In June 2017, the DOL made effective a new rule, known colloquially as the Fiduciary Rule that expanded the scope of the fiduciary standard of care under ERISA. Under the Fiduciary Rule, any financial professional providing investment advice to qualified plans, including participants and beneficiaries, for a fee or other compensation must act in the client's best interest, charge no more than reasonable compensation, and not make any misleading statements about investment transactions, compensation, and conflicts of interest. Although the fiduciary rule has been thrown out by the 5th Circuit Court of Appeals, this fiduciary discussion is far from over amongst the regulators.

Lastly, although not a regulator, the CFP® Board historically required a CFP® designee to operate as a fiduciary only when creating a financial plan. The Board has recently approved a new Code of Ethics and Standards of Conduct, effective October 1, 2019 where a CFP® will be required to be a fiduciary 100% of the time, as shown in Table 11.1.

Many consumers assume that the financial professional with whom they deal with is required to work in the best interest of the client, rather than to improve their own financial condition. They are surprised to find out this is not always the case. This seems horrifying since they seek financial advisors to increase their financial well-being. Imagine the lack of faith consumers would have if they thought medical doctors were not required to put their health in front of their own interest and recommend the absolute best solution they can conceive. If you knew a doctor was compensated only when he/she prescribed a particular drug, would you take that drug? Clients want their financial advisors to work in their best interest, and they want them to be fiduciaries. If we are as client focused as we say we are, then we must deliver on what clients are asking for, otherwise we are hypocrites.

Regardless of regulation, the first primary component of being a fiduciary is to ensure competency, which means being educated in everything you need to know and referring the client to someone else if their concerns are outside of your knowledge. Table 11.1, Panel B, shows the CFP Board supports this competency in full where the other regulations satisfy a perfunctory standard.

The second fiduciary requirement is to ensure trustworthiness—obliging to ongoing ethics education, pledging requirements, and disclosing all potential conflict of interest. The proposed CFP Board requirement for CFP® designees is the only provision that meets this consumer need. It provides the signal that this is someone they can trust in terms of competency and ethics. It is this fiduciary standard that will sanction financial advising as a profession that meets consumer expectation. Without CFP® commitment to this proposed standard, the consumer must understand the formula for a fiduciary.

Fiduciary = adviser working under the Adviser Act as an RIA + never switching hats to work under the SEC 1934 act (aka. dually registered) + holding a CFP® designation.

The National Association of Personal Financial Advisors (NAPFA) has tried to filter out true fiduciaries, defining them as "Fee-Only," but due to grandfather laws, advisors working under NAPFA, who are not CFP®s do not hold the competency component.

Mentor Insight: Your brand message includes your internal message within your firm and your external message to consumers. Technical competence and trustworthy behavior are qualities everyone supports. Consider how you incorporate these qualities into your brand messaging.

PRINCIPAL KNOWLEDGE

Core Skills

Both the CFP Board and the CFA Institute rely on a dynamic practice analysis process to ensure competencies for the profession. In conducting the analysis, both organizations define core competency skills with a focus on answering the following questions:

- What skills are firms and consumers demanding when hiring investment or financial advisor professionals?
- What are the common skill deficits of investment/financial advisor professionals at the early stages of their career?

- What regulatory changes are impacting the investment/financial advisor management practice?
- What are the emerging trends in the financial services profession?

Depending on the direction of your practice, it is important to know what each of these organizations has defined as core competency skills. For example, the CFP Board has captured 72 topics from their job task analysis that fall under eight principal knowledge topics. These topics are used to establish an educational curriculum for CFP® classes and the basis for the CFP® examination.

1. Professional Conduct and Regulation
2. General Principles of Financial Planning
3. Education Planning
4. Risk Management and Insurance Planning
5. Investment Planning
6. Tax Planning
7. Retirement Savings and Income Planning
8. Estate Planning

It is important to acquire these core skills which is automatically covered if you pursue the educational requirements for the CFP® designation.

Mathematical Aptitude

Women's confidence in their analytical skills continues to be challenged in most of the analytical professions, even when they have strong mathematical skills. Many women feel they are surrounded by men who appear to have more experience, confidence, technical competence, and analytical ability, even when it may not be true.[5]

There is quite a lot of research examining women's mathematical abilities and the causes for lower performance, confidence, and risk-taking.[6] The research shows there are no biological reasons for women to underperform in mathematics, but it continues to promote the idea that women are less confident or interested in their mathematical abilities—which seems to have a self-fulfilling prophecy.

Julie Nelson, the chairwoman of the economics department at the University of Massachusetts, Boston, challenged many of the studies, showing that you can't take all research at face value. She reviewed 24 papers that reported women as less likely to be confident in their mathematical abilities or to take financial

---

[5]Wilson, F. (2003). Can compute, won't compute: Women's participation in the culture of computing. *New Technology, Work and Employment*, 18(2), 127–142.

[6]For a meta-analysis, see Hyde et al. (1990).

risk. She found many of the researchers overgeneralized. The studies were either inaccurate or highly exaggerated.[7] She also posited that there may be a bias among the publications, most of which look for research that confirms biases.

Mentor Insight: Women need to fight the urge to allow anyone to tell them that they are less confident, less prone to financial risk and less capable at math. Women must simply not accept the limitations originated from social gender bias.

Overall, women tend to be more negative toward mathematical occupations, which have historically been associated with men. To make matters worse, some young women point to the fictionalized masculine images of finance (think of the extreme—*The Wolf of Wall Street* or the Showtime series, *Billionaire*). They believe this behavior is incompatible with their own feminine image and not attractive. But the image of finance is changing, and as more women enter the field, the change will accelerate.

Math is a necessary skill to have if you want to be taken seriously in the finance field. However, advanced math is not required. Basic algebra, business math, and statistics are sufficient to be a financial advisor. Math skills contribute to important critical thinking, decision-making, and problem-solving abilities. In any financial position, you must have good analytical skills to be able to identify, formulate, and solve problems in a systematic approach.

Mentor Insight: Mathematical capabilities are necessary for a career in financial services to calculate the present value of a loan, the future value of an investment, or the standard deviation of a fund. Math skills build confidence in your ability.

Economic Insight

Good technical skills include a solid understanding of economics and the ability to analyze the economic climate. Economics is the study of individual and firm behavior and the interrelationship between consumer financial decisions and government decisions, which influence production, distribution, and consumption of resources. Because economics impacts interest rates, taxation rates, prices of goods and services, and investment returns, it is important for a financial advisor to understand economic conditions and how the government uses economic information to create policy.

This is a continuous learning requirement since the environment is dynamic. Advisors should spend extra time, on an ongoing basis, understanding the economic climate and what it means to the markets and to the consumer.

Mentor Insight: Some advisors practice strategic asset allocation and market themselves as having an "all weather strategy," which is a strategy created to perform under different market conditions. Others simply adhere to a buy and

---

[7]Nelson, J. A. (2014). The power of stereotyping and confirmation bias to overwhelm accurate assessment: The case of economics, gender, and risk aversion. *Journal of Economic Methodology, 21*(3), 211–231.

hold philosophy maintaining that it doesn't matter what is currently happening. Sometimes these advisors develop a false sense of security and do not stay abreast of changing market conditions, which could be interpreted as not being in the client's best interest. Financial advisors should always be monitoring the "weather" since risk can be mitigated through vigilant monitoring.

The study of economics is broken into macroeconomics and microeconomics. Microeconomics is the study of how individuals and households make financial decisions to best use limited resources. It focuses on consumer spending, income needs, risk tolerance, and wealth building. It looks at the changing needs of the household over the life cycle. Mathematical constructs are used to understand rational financial decision making which maximize "utility." Another important principal in microeconomics is the concept of opportunity cost or the cost of forgoing the next best alternative. The theories behind bounded rationality and behavioral finance explore why rational decisions are shunned. The better understood, the more a financial advisor can help individuals avoid these mistakes.

Macroeconomics is the study of large economic factors that indicate where the entire economy is heading. Understanding how to interpret Gross Domestic Product (GDP), which is a measurement of the country's output, can help the financial advisor determine if the economy is expanding or contracting and assess the overall stability of the economy.

An understanding of inflation is important too because it can directly impact a client's wealth and their financial plan. The Consumer Price Index (CPI) measures inflation. The Producers Price Index (PPI) represents the cost of goods and services relative to prior periods and represents the value of money or the purchasing power of a dollar.

Employment numbers are important to monitor as well, since employment can stimulate inflation or identify other problems with the economy. Financial advisors also need to understand how the demand and supply of loanable funds affect interest rates, which could impact major purchasing decisions as well as investments.

Mentor Insight: A financial advisor who understands and utilizes economic information will be better prepared to interpret the actions of the Federal Reserve, in terms of monetary policy and Congress in terms of fiscal policy. This prepares you to make better recommendations and increases the probability of a client's success. If nothing else, your client may understand aspects of this topic and would like your assessment. It is important to connect with your client on this topic since it builds confidence in your knowledge.

Critical Thinking Skills

High on the list of abilities necessary for success in the financial services sector are critical thinking and decision-making skills, which are gained through practice and experience. You cannot improve these skills by thinking harder;

it's about thinking more effectively. These skills are deliberate and are at the heart of conscious engagement.

Understanding your own biases can help to develop critical thinking skills. Judgment can be subjective and is usually based on assumptions, as we have learned in behavioral finance classes and this book. A second way to develop critical thinking skills is to think strategically about your next move and all of the possible consequences of your actions along the way. Working on your own strategic career plan is a great way to develop and hone your critical thinking skills.

Mentor Insight: Critical thinking is important when solving difficult or complex problems. Question your assumptions and be aware of your mental shortcuts that bias and prejudice your decisions. Many people find reversing the problem helpful. Start with the end in mind and remain focused on your vision.

Communication Skills

Communication skills are essential. You can be the best critical thinker in the world but if you can't share your thoughts; you become ineffective. Knowledge sharing starts with listening, understanding nonverbal cues, and empathizing with your client's situation. Only then can you determine if your ideas will be helpful. Communicate your ideas in a way that inspires the other person to take action. Your thoughts only matter if they influence someone to take action. Of course, trust facilitates the communication process. (Communication and trust building are discussed further in Chapter 13.)

Both written and oral communication skills are important, as well as business presentation skills. Effective presentation skills reduce miscommunication, which is likely the biggest cause of work-related problems. These skills will help you sell your ideas to your internal stakeholders and your clients.

Business Development Skills

Often when an advisor first starts working in the financial services industry, they will begin as a paraplanner or an associate financial advisor. Those roles require technical competency and communication skills to develop relationships with existing clients. As you progress in your career, business development skills bring in new revenue, which helps to grow the business and your compensation.

Business development skills are not so different than the skills you have already been working on to be successful within your firm and with clients. As you learn to communicate and influence your clients to take action, you'll also learn to negotiate and persuade new clients to work with you. If you believe in your services and the value you offer, the ability to convince people to join your firm becomes much easier. This is the difference between selling something to someone they may or may not need and offering your services, which have the potential to improve their lives.

Senior Management

At the highest ranks, when you become a partner or a senior manager at the firm, a plethora of other business skills is required. Advisors who developed their technical skills while completing a business degree with a bachelorette or masters in business administration will be more prepared to step into a senior role. In this role, you will be required to make decisions, to multitask, and to prioritize. The skills used in high-level positions are very different than those used as a financial advisor. Leadership and motivational skills that inspire others are incremental skills of particular importance when in a senior role.

Other Skills

Depending upon your business model and role within a firm, you must be able to use technological software and other tools. Developing research and project management skills to remain organized and focused are helpful. You need to understand your professional responsibilities to your clients, your firm, and the industry and adhere to ethical behavior. Although this is not a comprehensive list of all the additional skills you might need, a good attitude, work ethic, and enthusiasm are essential for a trained financial professional.

Employment and Technical Skills

You want to be "the right person on the bus," as Jim Collin's discusses in his book, *From Good to Great*.[8] Companies that first focus on having the right people on their staff are the most successful. Being the "right person" is fundamental for your success, which translates to finding a job where you can demonstrate your strengths, so you shine. When choosing an employer, you want to know what their core values are and if they are aligned with yours.

Mentor Insight: When women gain the technical skills required to be a financial professional and promote their brand through conscious engagement, they will add more value to their firm and clients, have more confidence and gain a higher measure of respect from other professionals in the business. Why not give yourself the tools to succeed?

EXERCISE: YOUR BRAND MESSAGE

It takes three seconds to form a first impression. In the workplace, your colleagues, senior executives, and subordinates will first observe your most obvious features—the way you dress, what you look like, your energy level, and your gender—to form an opinion about you. The initial impression

---

[8]Collins, J. C. (2001). *Good to great: Why some companies make the leap ... and others don't.* New York, NY: Harper Business.

can change as people get to know you and better understand your values, strengths, and passions. This requires networking to create relationships.

If you have worked in business for any length of time, you've most likely heard about a 30 second elevator pitch to capture prospect attention. Financial advisors need this type of pitch, but internal messaging is also important to communicate your unique value proposition to your firm's key employees. These are the people you need to buy into supporting your success. They are your stakeholders. In essence, you are selling your brand to them.

Just like an elevator speech, your brand message needs to be short. You should be able to communicate your entire value proposition in 60 seconds. It needs to be very clear and concise with simple to understand ideas that most people can immediately identify with. Be sure to express your vision and your passion. It should be compelling and tell the listener why they should care. The message should explain why your vision is important to them. It should leave no doubt about what you stand for or that you are genuine in your endeavor. The response that you want from your listener is, "that makes sense, and I want to learn more."

Your brand is your reputation—the perception held by the people you work with. To define your brand, you need to start with your:

1. Career values and reason for choosing a career in financial services (which you explored in Chapter 2).
2. Your top strengths and brand attributes (which you identified in Chapter 3).
3. Your beliefs (from Chapter 4).
4. Your vision and your strengths (from Chapters 5 and 9).
5. How your strengths align with the opportunities at the firm (from Chapter 6).

Summarize what you have learned about yourself. Select five adjectives you would use to describe yourself, for example, enthusiastic, friendly, and entrepreneurial. Ask trusted friends and family to help you. Would they use the same adjectives to describe you? After discussions, you may want to change the five adjectives to reflect a more comprehensive perspective.

1._____
_____
_____

2._____
_____
_____

3._____
_____
_____

4._____
_____
_____

5._____
_____
_____

Now, select five adjectives that you wish to portray. It's okay if they don't match what you listed above but with one caveat: They must be consistent with what you have identified about yourself. Your brand must represent your genuine identity.

1._____
_____
_____

2._____
_____
_____

3._____
_____
_____

4._____
_____
_____

5._____
_____
_____

What types of actions do you need to take to more strongly communicate the second set of adjectives? These actions may become part of your goals.

1._____
_____
_____

2._____
_____
_____

3._____
_____
_____

4._____
_____
_____

5._____
_____
_____

Summarize your unique value proposition (as you wish to portray it) to communicate to your stakeholders and other interested supporters.

_____

_____
_____
_____
_____
_____
_____
_____
_____
_____
_____
_____

Practice the message with people you trust (such as your advocacy circle which is discussed in the next chapter). Ask them what questions they have and what they think is missing.

Rework—this is an iterative process, and you will find ways to tweak the message.

CHAPTER 12

Advocacy Circle—Develop Your Brand

I met Elizabeth at a local FPA chapter meeting. She has been a member of a peer-to-peer group that has been operational for over twenty years. Elizabeth is in the long-term care field, which is the one area of financial services where women had an earlier penetration. Since women live longer than men, they recognize long-term care as primarily a female concern.

Elizabeth's group was made up of like-minded women in the field who wanted to help women prepare to live the end of their life in dignity and comfort. She talks about this group like they are family. She recounts times in her life where her "sisters" helped her make decisions when she was stuck.

One such time was when she was thinking of changing her focus and going into another line of financial services. She explained to the group that she had two options. The first was to continue selling long-term care. Even though she was an expert, she was loosing her passion and not enjoying it any longer. Her other option was to go back to school to become a Certified Financial Planner, which meant being in school for two years and sitting for the CFP® examination.

Elizabeth's peer group helped her make the decision. One question that came from the group changed everything: What would it take to rekindle your passion in the long-term care space? Elizabeth hadn't even thought about ways to reinvigorate her old career, she just thought it was time to get out. They brainstormed what she could do.

What she liked about becoming a Certified Financial Planner was the idea that she could spend more time educating her clients and helping them versus selling them products. The group helped her reshape her business, which changed from a transactional business to a relational business where she educates her clients and is their trusted advisor. She now writes articles for various publications, has published a book, and speaks at events where she encourages CFP®s to prepare their female clients for this vulnerable period in their lives. Elizabeth is reinvigorated and she has her peer-to-peer group

© The Author(s) 2018
L. Mattia, *Gender on Wall Street*,
https://doi.org/10.1007/978-3-319-75550-2_12

to thank for giving her a different perspective and helping her to explore her options.

As Elizabeth told me, being a member of a peer-to-peer group was like having her own personal board and is even better than a personal coach or mentor. "I get so many different ideas and I see how members of the group build on each other's ideas. The end result is better than what one person could have thought of. This is a case where the mastermind (our collective minds) is operating at a much higher level than each of our individual minds. This group has become one of the most important relationships in my life and I am forever committed to the collective group."

Several years ago, I was involved with an Advocacy Circle that served women going through a divorce. Jean was a Certified Divorce Financial Analyst who worked with couples to mediate their divorce. She had written a book, which she pitched to one of the large publishing houses. They liked her book but wanted her to come up with a better title. Jean spent all weekend coming up with thirty possible titles. She submitted the titles, and they rejected all of them. She came up with thirty more, and they rejected those too.

When Jean brought the book title issue to the circle, she was at her wits end. She felt she was completely out of ideas. The circle helped her brainstorm and came up with thirty fresh ideas. Ultimately, the publisher selected one of the circle's ideas and it was something Jean would have never thought of.

An Advocacy Circle serves numerous functions. Primarily, it provides a support structure of like-minded individuals who are committed to your success. It holds you accountable to your goals and helps you think through your options when working toward a solution. The benefit of working with an Advocacy Circle are many, but here is a list of what I consider the top ten benefit:

1. Accountability to think ahead and plan for the next meeting, acting upon your plan.
2. Feedback and constructive criticism from others who want to see you succeed—you no longer are "alone."
3. Membership to an exclusive community where members rely on each other and care about each other's success.
4. Network and connectivity beyond the members—expanding your network exponentially by gaining access to the other member's networks.
5. Achievements of collaboration where the circle works together to achieve objectives.
6. Expansion of knowledge and understanding by sharing the unique skills and experiences of circle members. Gain insights you might not have otherwise gained.
7. Promotional opportunities to assist with each other's businesses.
8. Encouragement to think bigger than you ever have.
9. New resources and specialty areas of knowledge.
10. Motivation to grow and avoid stagnation.

MENTORS: THE MAGIC BULLET?

Sally approached me at a seminar for financial advisors hosted by a large RIA firm. She was unhappy with her mentor. "He wants me to do all these extra things outside of my job responsibilities. He keeps telling me that I need to gain more visibility. I'm on a bunch of task teams and other committees, and I'm working myself to death. In the meantime, when I really needed him to step-up and support me for a position working on the bond desk, he told me that he didn't think I was qualified for the position. I have a degree in economics and have passed the first CFA® exam. It turns out the man who got the job had a degree in biology and no other qualifications. He certainly was not more qualified. Is this mentor really helping me?"

Unfortunately, this was not the first time I heard this type of complaint. Mentoring means different things to different people. If the mentor has no power or commitment to your success, his or her help will be limited. Some women feel their mentors create a lot of work with no reward. Fundamentally, having a mentor is like having a trusted advisor who is available to support and advise you when you need it. A mentor should be someone who cares about you and always has your best interests in mind. Ideally, the mentor acts as a sponsor, which means they go beyond providing feedback and advice and are able to operate as your advocate, promoting you for new opportunities and promotions.

A recent *Harvard Business Review* article highlights a problem with mentorship. When women did have "sponsor" mentors, the mentors were not committed enough to take the risk of advocating for the woman to fill a traditionally male-dominated role.[1] Again this lack of commitment continues to haunt women. The 2008 Catalyst Survey showed that women have more mentors than men but the relationships had little influence on career movement.[2] The survey identified that some women had more than four mentors. This implies a superficial relationship and the question arises: What level of quality was the mentorship? Could the relationships be deep and committal? What type of value can be created by superficial relationships without authority, power, or a genuine commitment to advocate and support the mentee? It doesn't make sense. How could that scenario work?

Mentors are often found within the same company. They should serve as a career advisor and advocate. They should help reinforce how a mentee's job contributions fit into their long-term career goals, and perhaps even how they fit into the bigger picture of the company's goals. Some companies have career mentorship programs as part of a person's development strategy. These programs work best when the mentor is a volunteer, someone who is interested in providing this type of support. If you work with a mentor, you will

---

[1] https://hbr.org/2010/08/women-are-over-mentored-but-un.

[2] Ibarra, H., Carter, N. M., & Silva, C. (2010). Why men still get more promotions than women. *Harvard Business Review, 88*(9), 80–85.

want to take advantage of their advice but it does not preclude you from also working with an advocacy circle that relies on committed peer mentorship outside your firm.

If you do not have a formal mentor program at your firm, finding a mentor can be daunting. It is a little like finding a boyfriend. It isn't the type of thing you should focus on; it will happen when the time is right. When you meet a mentor, you will know it. You will see that the person is invested in you, but how do you get people to invest in you? That is easy— just keep investing in your stakeholders, in your brand message, focus on your strengths, minimize your weaknesses, and have an aspirational vision... Are you getting it? If you go up to a guy and whine about the fact that you don't have a boyfriend, how attractive do you think you are? Instead, the way to find a boyfriend is by enjoying and living life, which is what makes you attractive. It's the same with senior executives: show your potential, sell them on your vision, and inspire your stakeholders. Make them want to invest in you.

Mentor Insight: Don't ask a stranger to be your mentor. It puts people in an awkward position. Even if they say yes, what ensures they are really going to devote the time and energy to help you be successful? Mentors are human too. They need to be inspired. In fact, they don't have control over you and they are taking a risk. Although they could gain pride and satisfaction from helping you, the upside is not great. You need to motivate them, to inspire them, and if you do, they will become immersed in your career.

At Travelport, I helped Kate gain her confidence but she also helped me. She had been at the company for a long time, and she knew how things worked. She went out of her way to make certain I was prepared for a presentation and to tell me where the problems were. She invested in my career as a mentor would. Being grateful and inspired by her potential, I reciprocated.

The hope is that senior women will help junior women in the same way that senior males help junior males get promoted. In order for this to happen, senior women must be available, capable, and committed to advocating for other women. After all, women have a proven core competency in relationship building so this networking capability should be second nature. Ironically, the female network has not developed as much as we would like, which we discussed in Chapter 9. With fewer women than men at the top levels, women can rely on an advocacy circle with peer mentors committed to your success.

Mentor Insight: Mentors can come from anywhere. Peers who experience the same difficulties can provide practical counsel. Even subordinates who know the secret to mastering a particular process or dealing with a specific client can provide valuable mentorship.

Peer Mentors

When I was asked to create a program to support female financial advisors at various stages of their career at Texas Tech University, I wanted to understand the women's career concerns. To learn what they were looking for, we ran focus groups made up of graduating seniors and already graduated alumni. The groups were lively. Both groups of women had shared several valuable insights and specifically, six core goals:

- To be prepared to succeed in the financial services industry.
- To better understand the profession's culture and unspoken rules.
- To strengthen and positions soft skills such as communication and negotiation by demonstrating sensitivity to adverse gender perceptions. (These women had already developed strong technical skills in the Personal Financial Planning degree program.)
- To develop a strategy that included goal setting, goal progress, and career management.
- To build their confidence and self-worth.
- To give back and support other women in their success.

In response to the feedback, we created a program called "Women Advocacy Circles." We used the term "advocacy" because we want women to commit their support to each other and influence each other's success within financial institutions. Advocacy is defined as "an activity by a group that aims to influence decisions within political, economic, and social systems and institutions." The goal of the Women Advocacy Circle is to advocate for all women—and more specifically, the women in your circle.

The advocacy circles have the potential to build, coach, and bring out each member's strengths as well as the group's collective strengths, counteracting any negative input that could obstruct career success. In a behavioral study looking at organizational teams, it was shown that positive interpersonal connections build psychological engagement and protective abilities that are robust against negative influences.[3]

Marcial Francisco Losada, a Chilean psychologist studied teams who were asked to develop a strategic plan. He found the more positive the team members, the more successful the team in their overall success as measured by the profitability of the business and evaluations given by colleagues and superiors. The teams that built their interpersonal connections on member's strengths were able to minimize the hidden challenges that could impede their success.

The Women Advocacy Circle concept encourages members to navigate around gender-related and other work place challenges. The structure of the

---

[3] Losada, M., & Heaphy, E. (2004). The role of positivity and connectivity in the performance of business teams: A nonlinear dynamics model. *American Behavioral Scientist, 47*(6), 740–765.

program is intentionally flexible. It is inherently dependent upon a Retreat where everyone gets acclimated and oriented to the nature of the program and develops relationships with their new Women Advocacy Circles. It is hoped that the circles are so successful they will continue to meet years after the initial retreat.

The program is designed to combine brainstorming, education, peer accountability, and support to sharpen business and personal skills. Participants are encouraged to challenge each other to set powerful goals, and more importantly, to accomplish them. The circle requires commitment, confidentiality, willingness to both give and receive advice and ideas, and support each other with total honesty, respect, and compassion.

Advocacy circle members act as catalysts for growth, devil's advocates, and supportive colleagues. This is the essence and value of the circles. Each member will gain insights to improve their business and personal life. Each Women's advocacy circle is an objective board of directors, a success team, and a peer-to-peer group, all rolled into one.

The weekend retreat is where we work on creating the circles with an emphasis on getting to know each other and building trust. We discuss the difficulties that still exist in the workplace and strategies to navigate around the difficulties. We also conduct soft-skill training around effective communication and negotiation skills. Most importantly, we discuss the structure, the rules, and the process regarding how the Women's Advocacy Circles will work over the next several months.

The Women Advocacy Circle meetings follows the retreat and takes on an agenda, which includes the following minimum components. These groups use a mastermind structure including the Hot Seat Method:

- Update—Each member updates the group on how they did accomplishing their goals from the previous meeting. The purpose here is not to go into too much detail or probe, but simply have accountability by vocalizing how you did.
- Hot Seat—A pre-selected member shares details about their situation and any problems or questions they have. The other members of the group then have the opportunity to provide specific help and advice for this individual.
- Goal Setting—A recap for each member to briefly state their goals for the next meeting.
- Hot Seat Selection—The next person to be in the "hot seat" is selected so they can come prepared with questions or concerns to bring before the group next time.

When people sit in the Hot Seat, sometimes they don't know how to frame their topic or question so the other members can follow. This leads to a rambling and disjointed Hot Seat presentation that confuses the other members.

The problem is that the members then spend the rest of the time asking questions in order to gain clarity and don't have enough time for actual brainstorming and problem solving. To avoid this problem, the Hot Seat presenter should ask themselves the following questions as they prepare for the meeting.

- Where do I feel stuck and what help do I want from my Advocacy Circle?
- How do I feel about the situation and what is the problem or situation I want to explore?
- How is the problem related to my goals and vision?
- What decision do I need to make and do I need to revise any of my goals?
- What have I tried already?

Advocacy Meetings

While there is no ideal number of circle members, we try to keep circle between five and seven people. With too many members, the meetings might be too long and there might not be enough time for people to get an equal opportunity to share and receive value. However, in the beginning, it may be unclear if everyone is committed. In an academic setting, if two out of seven people don't contribute, you still have a quorum for the meeting. A circle of four or five very committed individuals is ideal to receive valuable input.

The circles should decide upon:

- the precise meeting frequency, length, and timing
- set ground rules for membership and behavior during the meeting including language protocol
- should discuss circle expectations and how they align with individual expectations.

Doing this work upfront (ideally, at the retreat) affects decision making, promotes a sense of shared purpose, motivates circle members, recognizes the different member interests, reduces conflicts, and focuses on results and outcomes.

The circle should also define key roles by naming a leader, a timekeeper, and a host. The leader determines the agenda and makes certain the upcoming Hot Seat member or any presenters (if applicable) are prepared. The timekeeper keeps the meeting on schedule. The host arranges for physical or electronic meetings. Many advocacy circles (and other mastermind/peer groups) meet remotely for their regular meetings, but usually meet in person once a year (perhaps at a retreat type of event). If you plan to meet remotely, determine what software (Google Hangouts, Skype, or Zoom) the circle members prefer during the retreat so the logistics are established upfront.

Although having a facilitator is not always necessary and can create an additional expense, a facilitator can help with several tasks. They keep the circle on track, help resolve conflict, bring in extra exercises to help the circle grow and develop, manage new entrance and exits to the circle, help members make decisions and choose a course of action, enforce group guidelines, deal with problem members, and track group member progress. In fact, the facilitator can help find the ideal participants for the circle and create an application and screening process so that like-minded women are matched up with each other. If given a choice, it is best to start with a facilitator. You can always decide to go on your own in the future when the circle has become a cohesive group and you are clear about processes and expectations.

15 Ways to Be an Amazing Advocacy Circle Member

Lea, an Advocacy Circle participant told me, "I've been in a couple of mastermind groups in the past. When the members show up as they said they would we had productive meetings. But, when they allow other things to get in the way of their commitment to the group, our meetings became a complete waste of time."

She is absolutely right. There are circles that work and others that don't. The ones that work well are worth it and the reason they work is because the members are committed. The success of the circle has everything to do with the members and if you have a facilitator, it is their job to make sure you have the right members. As an advocacy circle peer mentor, you have a responsibility to yourself and to the members of your circle. The following guidelines can help you be an amazing advocacy circle member.

1. **Demonstrate your commitment.** In agreeing to participate you are agreeing to do your best to attend and be prepared for all the agreed sessions. It's not an open group where people come and go when they want. This is a circle that is committed to learning and growing together. We recognize that life happens and things come up so if someone is unable to make a session you are expected to notify whoever is leading that session.

2. **Agree to confidentiality,** which is crucial in establishing the supportive circle culture. Everything that is shared by others must be kept confidential. You can share your personal experience with other people but you must never discuss any of the other member's experiences. Every member is expected to keep everything people share in strict confidence.

3. **Mutual respect, kindness, and positive regard** are essential ingredients to creating a trusting environment where people feel safe to share, be vulnerable, and authentic. While it might seem obvious that everyone would do this, stating it as part of the circle agreement is

important to cultivate safety. Treat each other with respect and kindness, through open-minded listening.

4. **Time awareness** is encouraged, where all members are on time for circle meetings. If for some reason you are late, just come in quietly and sit down. If you know you will be late for any reason, please let the leader or facilitator know in advance because in most cases, they will be waiting for you and won't want to start without you. Your group is whole and complete when we are all together.

5. **Positive attitude,** which is a personal attribute required to be successful in financial services. By showing the other members what it takes to be productive and successful, members reinforce behaviors and actions required to succeed.

6. **Active listening,** which is easier said than done but developing this skill will also make you a better financial advisor. It means making a conscious effort to truly pay attention to what your circle members are saying, instead of thinking about what you're going to say next. You might worry that you need to come up with something helpful right away, when in fact, the best thing you can do for the other members is to listen closely to what they're saying, ask open questions to dig deeper, and act as a sounding board.

7. **Genuine Interest to learn** the values, vision, and goals that inspire each member in order to give excellent advice. You need to know each member of your group on a personal level to help them find success and gratification in the financial services profession. A good member is committed to empowering the other members to develop their strengths, their strategy, and relationships for success.

8. **Willingness to share your skills, knowledge, and expertise** to meet other members where they are in their professional development. At times you might be the expert in the room or the person with the most experience but as you share your knowledge, other members will add insights so that you gain a deeper awareness and clarity than if you kept it to yourself.

9. **Exhibit enthusiasm and optimism for female success in financial services** and commit to supporting women entering the profession. All members want to feel as if this career has meaning. Enthusiasm is contagious.

10. **Value ongoing learning and growth in the field** at different career stages. The financial services profession is growing and changing so even experienced members can learn new things. Anyone who feels stagnant in their current position will not make a good advocacy member. Good advocacy members are open to new learning practices. They continually read professional journals and may even write articles on subjects where they have developed expertise. They are excited to

share their knowledge with new people entering the field. They enjoy taking workshops and attending professional conferences provided through their membership in professional associations such as the Financial Planning Association (FPA) and the National Association of Personal Financial Planners (NAPFA).

11. **Provide guidance and constructive feedback** by asking questions and probing to fully understand the situation before giving advice and constructive feedback. An amazing member understands this is a big responsibility and does their best to provide as much value as she can.

12. **Give more than you ask for**. At the risk of sounding cliché, consider two popular and wise principals: "you only get what you put in" and "what goes around, comes around." As you selflessly offer your support, wisdom, and time, you will see the rewards in the success of your peers and their support for you.

13. **Focus on the long term** as if you'll be a circle member forever. This mind-set will make it easier for you to give long-term guidance, which will help each other's decisions even if the circle no longer exists.

14. **Be honest and open about mistakes you've made.** Sharing your own mistakes and failures helps for problem-solving purposes but also builds trust, and gives others permission to admit when they have made mistakes or when they are struggling.

15. **Lead by example.** Demonstrate these principals in every circle meeting, and always be engaged and ready to work.

CLOSURE/RESET

At some point, the members in your Advocacy Circle may decide it is time to check in with the process to determine if the group is working as planned or if changes need to occur. For the university program, we reconvene for an afternoon at the end of the semester to debrief and have a closing ceremony.

There are several reasons why it is important to go through a specific debrief process. Debriefing can highlight the circle's accomplishments, which might be overlooked or discounted in other situations. It uncovers any issues that require attention. The circle strengthens as a result of reflection, honest feedback, and wrestling with issues. Reflection, interpretation, and capturing the learnings for the future are the general steps.

Step 1: Reflecting: What happened with your Advocacy Circle?

- What happened?
- What did you observe?
- How did you feel?

Step 2: Interpreting: Why you experienced the circle the way you did?

- Is that what you expected?
- Why do you think that may have happened? Is there a general theme?
- What did you learn?
- What could have been done differently and how would it have changed the outcome?

Step 3: Applying the learning: How might this help you in the future?

- How do you think you could use these ideas in future circles, networks, or even your relationships at work?
- What needs to happen for these ideas to work?
- What possible problems do you need to be aware of?
- Where does the circle go from here?
- Where do you personally go from here?

THE WoMEN's MONEY EMPOWERMENT NETWORK (WoMEN)

The Women Advocacy Circles are another way I have worked on developing my personal vision. This is the vision that I discussed in Chapter 10: encouraging women to become engaged in household, corporate, and world finances for the greater good by empowering women in financial services to become leaders. They are an extension of the Women's Money Empowerment Network (WoMEN) started years ago to support women helping women with financial issues.

It began when I first realized women were still the minority in the room. Being a financial planner working with people to influence their lives is one of the most satisfying and inspirational careers a person can have. Yet, as a professor of financial planning, I had trouble getting female students excited. In fact, even when I taught corporate finance to the business students, more than a few female students told me that they were marketing majors so they didn't need to know finance. Really?

I kept thinking about the same nagging question that has haunted finance, financial services, the Certified Financial Planner Board, and the Charted Financial Analyst Institute for more than a decade. Why, almost sixty years after the woman's movement first began, is only 1 out of 5 CFP®s a woman, and why are even less CFA®s?

I decided I wanted to help women be more successful in the industry, which is why I founded, (WoMEN); a network of women financial services professionals providing support and opportunities for each other. The network is also intended to connect female financial professionals to women who are looking for compassionate and intelligent solutions—women who want the straight talk and empathy that women financial advisors offer. It is a network of women working with women.

The network is intended to work outside and around the financial institutions where female financial advisors have a voice and participate in defining the rules. All are invited to join. It's time women work together to support one another. Together we can improve lives. www.womensmoneyempowermentnetwork.com.

Mentor Insight: Network and create contacts inside the profession. Other women in finance are not your competition; they are your advocates and supporters. If they do well, we all do well and vice versa. If we as women in financial services ban together to lift each other up, there is no stopping us. I am not talking about unproductive protesting and collective complaining about why things don't change. I am talking about forming closer connections where we are able to advocate for each other, support each other's work, and ultimately, celebrate each other's wins.

WoMEN's Credo

In developing your circle's purpose and expectations, it might be helpful to consider a common credo. The WoMEN Credo is a set of beliefs that establish guidelines for the activities of Women Advocacy Circle. It serves as a reminder of why we have decided to work together. It is intended to motivate and lift our spirits. The essence of this book was created based upon this credo. It reflects our common values and the importance of women achieving successful careers in finance. It unites us in our collaboration to support and encourage all women in achieving their vision.

1. We have a strategy and a vision for our careers that is directly aligned with our values.
2. We are highly competent. We make certain that our technical skills in personal finance are broad and deep. We are continuous learners and make certain that we keep up with this dynamic and fast-paced industry.
3. We embrace mentoring and advocating and go out of our way to help other female financial professionals by supporting them to be successful.
4. We are aligned with our stakeholders: employers, partners, third party service providers, and suppliers. Through this alignment, we are able to better serve our clients and achieve greater success.
5. Our goals are S.M.A.R.T. and we manage the progress of our goals so they are achieved.
6. We focus on our strengths, which results in greater career happiness and a vicious cycle where we are fully and consciously engaged in our career.

7. We look for opportunities where we can fulfill our vision and make the highest contribution to the organizations where we work.

8. We are aware of our weaknesses and the threats to our careers and take steps to minimize our vulnerability while preparing our strategy. After that, we don't spend time thinking about these distractors and instead keep our eyes focused on our vision.

9. We are genuine in all of our relationships, with our clients, stakeholders, and circle members. We don't try to be something we are not. We value honesty and trust. We are loyal and will strive to always deliver. We are quick to own missteps and work diligently to turn everything right again.

10. We celebrate all female financial professional wins since a win for the individual is a win for all of us!

Self-Promotion Versus Promoting Other Women

The Women Advocacy Circles need to learn how to actively promote each other. As a peer mentor for the other woman in the circle, each member has their own unique strengths to help. Promoting each other builds trust and reinforces self-confidence. The more we can help each other the better since self-promotion can be tricky.

Nobody wants to be a doormat, and it is important to advocate for oneself. Promoting your accomplishments and speaking directly about your strengths is essential when other people don't know you well, especially if you are in competition for a well-positioned role, project, promotion, or simply a job. Self-promotion may be instrumental for managing perceptions and ensuring that others at work understand your competencies. It is usually considered a necessity for a job since it displays confidence and ambition. Yet, women who self-promote may suffer social reprisals for violating gender prescriptions.

Jessie Smith and Meghan Huntoon from Montana State University conducted a study into why women are uncomfortable talking about their accomplishments. They found that women who violate the "modesty gender norm" are evaluated harshly but if they promote others, they are evaluated favorably.[4]

Laurie Rudman from Rutgers University conducted three experiments that investigated the relationship between self-promotion and being hired. Her research showed that self-promotion reduced stereotypical thinking in terms of ability and led to higher competence ratings but at a cost where women were perceived to be less attractive socially.[5] Women especially don't like women who blatantly talk about their accomplishments.

[4] Smith, J. L., & Huntoon, M. (2014). Women's bragging rights: Overcoming modesty norms to facilitate women's self-promotion. *Psychology of Women Quarterly, 38*(4), 447–459.

[5] Rudman, L. A. (1998). Self-promotion as a risk factor for women: The costs and benefits of counterstereotypical impression management. *Journal of Personality and Social Psychology, 74*(3), 629.

The women in all three experiments hired self-promoting men over self-promoting women and preferred self-effacing women much more than self-promoting women. The problem is that perceived competence is correlated with both men and women who self-promote but there are repercussions for women who self-promote. This is another example of a double bind, which we discussed at length in Chapter 7.

Mentor Insight: If we are serious about the cause of promoting all women, we must learn to advocate for ourselves and for each other. We need to change the perspective that female recognition is a scarce resource and instead focus on creating opportunities for recognition and advocacy. A great way to start is with a Women's Advocacy Circle (peer-to-peer mentors).

One Last Comment—"Sexual Harassment"

Over time we hear women admitting they endured sexual harassment or assault in the workplace but were afraid to leave. I know this is also true in homes from the work I have done with domestic violence victims. It is heartbreaking. We must not tolerate anyone attempting to use their power to manipulate us in anyway. Of course, like most women I have experienced inappropriate advances. In fact, there is a primary reason why I left one of the organizations where I worked but I don't care to discuss (it would create a legal mêlée that I have no time for). In my mind, there is only one option when something egregious happens and that is to leave. In this particular case, the executives of the organization were very aware why I left. I filed my complaint with the head of HR and they had their lawyers lined up waiting for my salvo. Frankly, if I had fought, it could have made the front page of the newspaper but it wasn't worth it. I took my marketable and very valuable skills and I left. It was their loss. I voted with my feet. That has always been my philosophy. Just make sure you have options. When you don't like the treatment (irrespective of whether it is related to overt sexual harassment or just plain covert gender bias), you leave.

But listening to these women confirms what we already know. Women don't have confidence, have not built up their strengths or marketable skills and think they must stay and put up with inappropriate behavior. They don't advocate for themselves. And after what we discussed in this book, women who advocate for themselves are in danger of not being liked, a further deterrent. We need to support other women to advocate, self-promote, and speak up so we end these threats to our careers and our well-being.

So sure we can rise up and demand an end to this behavior. It is about time we pass the Equal Rights Amendment and enforce laws against sexual assault. But we all know regulation only goes so far. Let me remind you in 1964 the Civil Rights Act was passed prohibiting employment discrimination based on race, color, sex, religion, or national origin. In 1986, the Supreme Court ruled that sexual harassment can be sex discrimination. In 1991, more protection against discrimination in the workplace was added giving the right for plaintiffs to collect compensatory and punitive damages. Yet here we are.

We need to arm women with tools to fight back. We need to encourage *all* women whether they are headed for financial roles or for Congress, whether they are young girls or mature women to become STARs in their pursuit, to advocate for themselves and to surround themselves with a group of women, an Advocacy Circle, who will promote them. Imagine if every woman stood up and said, "NO, I HAVE A CHOICE. I DON'T HAVE TO TAKE IT ANY MORE. I'M OUT OF HERE."

Mentor Insight: This assumes you are unable to navigate around the behavior and/or you tried to stop it by standing firm, voicing your opposition and alerting others at your firm. Of course you can also take legal action. The point is that you don't need to tolerate or reinforce their power. Please be aware that pursuing legal action while remaining at the firm can be challenging and distracting. Only you can decide how harmful the environment is to your well-being. Since you have marketable skills that are wanted elsewhere, often the ideal choice is to leave and remain focused on your vision. How do we take back the power? Stop participating.

EXERCISES: WOMEN'S ADVOCACY CIRCLE PROGRESS REPORT

Member:	Date:	Last Meeting:

Personal Vision (rarely changes):

A. Annual Goals (tied to your strategic career plan; changes infrequently)

1.
2.
3.

B. Actions/Goals achieved – YTD

1.
2.
3.

C. Actions/Goals completed last period: (Results since last board meeting)

1.
2.
3.

D. Actions/Goals to complete for next period: (Deliverables by next board meeting);

1.
2.
3.

E. New Challenges/Opportunities/Changes in Environment: (Internally/externally that influence your decision making)

F. My question and/or Critical Issue this month is: (Or, what support or input do I need from the board)

G. By way of background the Board should know: (Relevant to the Critical Issue above; provides the context)

CHAPTER 13

Relationships—Share Your Brand

Martha was tasked with fixing her firm's inefficient operational process, which was thought to be the reason why it was so difficult to onboard and retain clients. She told me how the owner had given this project to her out of desperation since he just couldn't seem to fix it himself. He had tried before and often found that internal disagreements prevented the organization from making forward progress.

I suggested that Martha first do a stakeholder analysis to better understand the politics around the problem. She identified five key stakeholders, which can be seen in the sample stakeholder analysis at the end of Chapter 8. Her boss, Jack, thought the reason clients were leaving was due to the market's poor performance. Martha spoke to him about developing a communication plan for the clients. Although he agreed with the idea, he wasn't sure how it would be implemented.

As Martha explored key shareholder concerns and motives, she found the top advisors were frustrated by the lack of information they received from the investment committee. Both the founder of the firm and the office manager were concerned about inefficiencies and poor cooperation. The Chief Investment Officer felt underappreciated and thought his team did not receive the recognition they deserved in light of their ability to protect portfolios in a volatile investment environment.

Martha was clear. The overarching problem across the firm was due to poor communication. She started with the owner and discussed the firm's strategic plan. She knew he had developed one with the team because they went on an off-site retreat earlier in the year. She asked about the status of the plan. Jack told her, "There were a lot of great ideas but we ran out of time and didn't prioritize the them."

Martha talked to Jack about the problems they were having and how a strategic approach could help guide them. He agreed and asked her to lead the discussion. Before any formal meetings, Martha spent individual time

© The Author(s) 2018
L. Mattia, *Gender on Wall Street*,
https://doi.org/10.1007/978-3-319-75550-2_13

with each stakeholder, discussing what a strategic plan would do for them. Many of their comments were similar in nature but had a nuance that appealed to each person. When the list was finally presented at the first strategic meeting, each stakeholder saw the ideas as their own and of course thought they were brilliant.

By doing the preparatory work with each stakeholder, Martha was able to gain consensus with the group. In doing so, she solved the firm's primary problem (communication), while building relationships that would serve her well in the future. Her performance review reflected a job well done since all the stakeholders became her advocates. That is the power of a good stakeholder analysis; it cements the relationships you will need at some point in your career.

How to Build Trust

Look at your stakeholder analysis from the exercise at the end of Chapter 8. The objective of the analysis is to guide you in developing a trusting relationship with each of your stakeholders. You want each stakeholder to know what you stand for. This is where your brand message comes in. You want to communicate the essence of your brand, which is moderated slightly to connect with each person individually. Adjustments should be minor. You are not changing who you are just for one stakeholder. Remember, you want to be consistent at all times. You do not want to communicate one brand essence to one person and another to a different stakeholder.

Determine what you need from that stakeholder and what else, aside from your brand message, you need to communicate. Communicate what you want the other person to do, why it is important and what outcome you expect which is referred as the "What, So What, Now What" technique. You need to address who you are, why the other person should care, and what you are hoping to accomplish with the other person. The key to delivering this message is to always speak from the heart with integrity, honesty, and authenticity. Incidentally, in order to build trust, you have to let go of any unconscious bias that you may be holding onto that could prevent open dialogue. Consider whether you have a stereotype or preconceived idea about the stakeholder.

To ensure you are fully addressing your stakeholder's needs, ask them open questions as opposed to questions that elicit a yes or no answer. Summarize, reflect, and clarify back to the stakeholder what you think they said. This gives you both an opportunity to rectify any misunderstandings quickly. As the conversation moves forward, refer back to what the other person previously said. Look for incidents or examples of when you have both had common experiences. Demonstrate that you understand how the other person feels and sees things from their point of view. These are all techniques to build trust. When setting out to build trust with your stakeholders, look for as many ways of connecting as possible.

Mentor Insight: Take advantage of your inherent strength as a relationship builder. Women are natural networkers but I suspect the uncomfortable situation in the workplace may deter relationship building. Another possibility is that some women feel time constraints so they don't leverage relationships like the men do. Relationship building is a key part of your job and critical to your success.

RELATIONSHIP BUILDING

Case Study: Maria Bartiromo

Maria Bartiromo was the first female journalist to report from the NY Stock Exchange. She was pushed and yelled at, but she stayed focused on the prize. When she first started reporting, men spoke about her in condescending language. They discussed parts of her physiology as if her presence on the stock exchange floor was tantamount to her dancing at a gentlemen's bar (and as if they had permission to evaluate her in that way). It was disgusting, but Maria did not flinch. She stayed the course, and her strategic plan eventually gave her the visibility to become a financial leader.

In 2007, she had a setback that had the potential to crush her career. A controversy embroiled around a relationship she developed with a man at one of the large banks. Instead of recognizing her professional abilities, rumors began to spread that the relationship was a reason for her success, which implicated her credibility and her ethics.

Fortunately, she did not have to defend herself. The entire management team at CNBC had her back and put an end to the discussion.[1] They labeled the rumors and chatter as chauvinistic and inappropriate. Certainly, men use their relationships all the time to contribute to their success. The fact that Maria's management team immediately rallied to her defense says a lot about her ability to develop trusting relationships with her colleagues. *Her brand message and relationships did the work for her.*

As a result, Maria enjoys tremendous respect and recognition. She is financially rewarded, and she has a sense of achievement. Not only is she achieving financial rewards for herself and her family, but Maria is also a role model for women everywhere. She encourages them to become financially engaged and take control over their lives. She is a pioneer for female financial advisors and is paving the way for more female financial leaders.

---

[1] http://archive.fortune.com/2007/02/16/magazines/fortune/cnbc_citi.fortune/index.htm.

Case Study: Janet Yellen

Janet L. Yellen took office as Chair of the Board of Governors for the Federal Reserve on February 3, 2014, for a four-year term ending in 2018. She served as Chairman of the Federal Open Market Committee, the system's principal monetary policy-making body. Prior to her appointment as Chair, Dr. Yellen served as Vice Chair of the Board of Governors, where she simultaneously began a 14-year term as a member of the Board that will expire on January 31, 2024.

Dr. Yellen has impeccable credentials, which include being a Professor Emeritus at the University of California, Berkeley. She is a member of both the Council on Foreign Relations and the American Academy of Arts and Sciences. As the first woman to chair the central bank, she is a pioneer and contributes to the future of women in the financial services industry. Where Maria Bartiromo is highly visible in the media, Janet Yellen has been highly visible in the educational and political arena, both nationally and internationally, and her influence over American monetary policy has been noteworthy.

Janet Yellen was not appointed to her position without hesitation.[2] Despite her impeccable credentials and being the most qualified person, there were rumors that she was not up for the task and she was almost not appointed. There were never any specifics to support why she might be incapable of the role, but the allegations suggest overt gender bias. Fortunately, she was not left to advocate for herself. Instead, dozens of lawmakers signed a petition advocating for her. She also received tremendous support from various women's groups. Her success is evidence of the power of women supporting other women, not simply because she is a woman, but because she is a highly qualified woman. *Her brand message and relationships did the work for her.*

Janet Yellen is financially rewarded and is highly respected and recognized. She has served as an ethical role model for the industry where she asserted her power with easy logic and common sense. She has demonstrated unwavering direction and guidance in the financial domain and in the highest political arena.

Case Study: Liz Ann Sonders

Liz Ann Sonders is Senior Vice President and Chief Investment Strategist for Charles Schwab and Co., where she analyzes and interprets the economy and markets on behalf of Schwab's clients. She also provides written reports, audio and video recordings, conference calls, and webcasts. She is a regular contributor to Schwab's publications and the keynote speaker at many of the company's corporate and client events. She has provided responsible financial

[2] http://www.huffingtonpost.com/2014/01/06/janet-yellen-womens-group_n_4549907.html.

guidance to millions of Americans through the media. Her ability to break down complex financial concepts in a clear and articulate fashion has certainly grown her followers.

Liz Ann did not skate through her career without at least one episode of gender bias that could have hampered her potential influence. Although she was the most qualified person to represent her firm on television, she was almost passed over because she was a woman. Fortunately, a fellow colleague spoke up on her behalf and went straight to the head of the firm. He stood up for her and advocated for her. *Her brand message and relationships did the work for her.*

In 2008, Liz Ann was honored by the Girl Scouts of New York as an "Exceptional Role Model for Young Women." She has been a great role model, speaking to middle America about the dangers of stock picking, the need to diversify, and passive investing through ETFs and index funds. She empowers and educates women throughout the country to rationally invest in the market. She encourages sensible behavior, and she is an inspiration for all women—from young ladies in the Girl Scouts to female financial advisors.

For all three women, their reputations and their relationships were key to their success. Women are good at relationships, yet, for some reason, in financial institutions there seems to be a breakdown. Obstacles distract us from our vision, and they sabotage our efforts to create solid relationships that can support our success.

For me, a pivotal point came when I was working at Mars in the international assignment. My entire tenure at the company was challenging but I stuck in there and built my brand message and relationships. Many people thought the international assignment was glamorous because I got to fly all over the world. As time went on, it became increasingly difficult to see my children because of my travel schedule and it stopped working for me. My work–life became unbalanced.

I spoke to the President of M&M/Mars about my conflict, and Paul quickly assured me he would help out. He created a position for me back at the Hackettstown office to reengineer the facilities around the business processes. I moved my family back to New Jersey and attacked the assignment with diligence and gratitude. It was an interesting and challenging job, and I enjoyed it. It was important that I validate Paul's generosity and reciprocate his efforts on my behalf with a quality performance and a job well done. *This opportunity came about as a result of my brand message and relationships.*

Mentor Insight: A rewarding and satisfying career is attainable if you adequately prepare yourself to get past the challenges and focus on your strategic plan. The key components to your strategy must be to build your brand identity and reputation and develop trusting relationships. At some point in your career these pillars of your strategy are going to be your lifeline to ensuring your success.

Establishing Rapport

To achieve trust and strengthen your work relationships, you need to actively practice rapport building. When you are out of rapport with someone, it is impossible to create trust. A simple way to start is to look for common likes or dislikes. Most people build rapport with people like themselves; oftentimes, this is a feeling and not necessarily obvious commonalities. Think of someone you like: Do you see commonalities between you and that individual? Now, think of someone you don't like: Do you see commonalities between you and that individual? Good ways to build rapport are to be friendly and approachable without trying too hard, using people's names early in a conversation to connect, showing interest in the other person's work or something that is important to them, or complimenting their work.

Although most of us think of using words to build rapport, most rapport building occurs through nonverbal communication. The majority of rapport building comes from tone of voice, facial expressions, eye contact, and body movement.[3] Most people are unaware of these nonverbal cues and the effect they have on our ability to build rapport. Once you are aware, you can improve rapport by how you physically present yourself. Maintain a physical presence that is non-intimidating and approachable. Demonstrate interest by leaning toward the person you are talking to. Keep your hands open and your arms and legs uncrossed. Make eye contact. Nodding and making encouraging sounds while listening also signals that you are hearing what the speaker is saying.

A more contrived technique used to cultivate rapport uses both verbal and nonverbal cues to model someone with whom you want to build rapport. "Mirroring" creates a feedback loop that can facilitate awareness and communication. It is a way to develop intuition into what the other person is thinking and feeling, and it is a way of establishing a connection. Be cautious with this technique because the ability to match and mirror what the other person does without mimicking them can be difficult and requires practice. Simple gestures, such as sitting the same way they are sitting, can be a way to align with the other person. If their legs are crossed at the ankle, cross your legs at the ankle or if they have one arm on the table, place your own arm on the table too.

I use a mirroring exercise at the Advocacy Circle retreat where I ask the women to partner up with someone they don't know. I then ask partner B to leave the room and tell partner A that when partner B returns, they should discuss the retreat, their assessment of the experience, and what they hoped to get out of the program. While engaged in conversation, they should try to match and mirror their partner.

[3] https://www.psychologytoday.com/blog/beyond-words/201109/is-nonverbal-communication-numbers-game.

Upon partner B's return, partner A begins to subtly mirror their partner's physiology (including voice tone, volume, and tempo). About ten minutes into the conversation, I ask partner B how they feel about the overall conversation and if they agree with their partner. Almost every time, partner B says they were enjoying the conversation and completely concurred with their partner. I then ask them to notice if they are sitting in the same posture, using the same types of gestures, speaking at a similar speed and volume, or in a similar voice tone range, as the other person. Once I point out the similarities, some participants even observed they had been breathing together and others felt they were communicating on an instinctual level. These experiences are not uncommon and have been scientifically proven to be effective.

Mentor Insight: While practicing rapport building techniques, make sure you are comfortable and not forced. As you practice, it will become more comfortable. When in public places, observe other people's interaction and take note of body postures and non-verbal cues that demonstrate rapport.

EFFECTIVE NEGOTIATIONS

Do you consider yourself an expert negotiator? If you weren't, you wouldn't be as successful as you are today and you would not be reading this book. Everything you have done in your life up until today has been a negotiation. Conversations are a give and take. Many people think negotiations are win-lose, but the most successful negotiations are designed to be a win-win for both parties.

Think about going into a car dealership and haggling over the price of a car. In this situation there is a disparity of power and information asymmetry where you have less information than the car salesperson. It is always better if you have done your homework, but even then, the imbalance is still felt, and most of us don't like it. If you find yourself on either end of a negotiation process where you feel you have either won or lost (relative to the other person), the negotiation has not been optimal.

In the workplace, there is no such thing as a single negotiation. Single interactions set the stage for follow-up interactions, both with the person you are negotiating with and the other people who have observed your negotiation abilities. These interactions affect your brand message and reputation, which you should carefully guard whenever you negotiate. You always want to know your end goal, what you want from the relationship, and ideally what the other person wants. Hopefully, you have already started developing your understanding of the other person by creating a stakeholder analysis.

To complicate the negotiation process, women are often concerned they will be perceived as either out for themselves or as a pushover. It is widely acknowledged that women don't negotiate when advocating for themselves for higher compensation or other non-pecuniary job-related items, including being considered for more challenging positions. It has also been shown that women avoid negotiations to minimize being socially penalized. They are concerned about deviating from expectations of proper feminine behavior. They are also concerned that "proper feminine behavior" communicates a lack of power and leadership, which is detrimental to their brand. We have discussed the difficulty that women experience in finding a balance. The key is to focus on being rational, fair, and trustworthy.

Mentor Insight: The most important part of negotiation is making the decision that you are willing to negotiate and understanding that if you don't negotiate, you are diminishing your value and you risk being seen as inferior.

Compensation negotiations are one type of negotiation which has been shown to be difficult for women. Hannah Riley Bowles and Linda Babcock, from Harvard University, tested strategies to help women improve their compensation negotiation skills while maintaining a positive brand reputation.[4] In the first study, they found that when women communicated the legitimacy of their request, they were more successful with the negotiation. They legitimized the salary request by producing another job offer as evidence of their value. This demonstrated thoughtfulness and logical reasoning, which keeps the conversation focused on the practicality of the request rather than the personal traits of the requestor. In this situation, the women used a third-party validation of their worth.

In their second study, the researchers found that by discussing their job request in terms of how it related to others in the organization it increased their colleagues' desire to work with them and also positioned the request as legitimate. In this study, the participants used a script expressing concern for organizational relationships that reinforced the women's concern for the company and the collective well-being of the employees. The request was positioned in two different ways. The first justification for the request was that their supervisor advised them to pursue the request, implying that the supervisor thought this was best for the department. The second justification for the request was to highlight their ability to negotiate as an important requirement of the job by saying, "I'm hopeful you'll see my skill at negotiating as something important I bring to the job." Again the key is to have a rationale for the request that focuses on the business need.

Mentor Insight: Explaining the legitimacy of the negotiation request in terms that are consistent with concern for the organization improves the outcome of the negotiation request while maintaining a positive brand reputation. Reframing the discussion as solving a problem takes the discussion away from appearing personal. Women are more effective when they consciously engage a collaborative, relational framing. For example, explaining why the request would be good for

---

[4]Bowles, H. R., & Babcock, L. (2013). How can women escape the compensation negotiation dilemma? Relational accounts are one answer. *Psychology of Women Quarterly, 37*(1), 80–96.

the team and improve the working relationship is better than only explaining why the request is good for you.

Another technique in negotiation, when women don't want to be perceived as aggressive, domineering, or competitive, is to focus on the win-win solution. This involves understanding the optimum solution for both parties. When negotiating an agreeable solution, it is good to know all of your options as well as all of the other person's options so you know where you have leverage.

Roger Fischer & William Ury conducted a well-known study around effective negotiation. They discuss the need to know each party's breaking point which is the least acceptable terms you are willing to agree upon. This is where both parties consider their best alternative to a negotiated agreement (BATNA).[5] Your BATNA is the most advantageous alternative course of action you can take if the other person refuses to negotiate with you. At the same time that you are reviewing your alternatives, you should also consider the alternatives available to the other party and what their BATNA is.

Sometimes the other party may be overly optimistic about their options, but the more you can learn about them, the better prepared you will be for negotiating in a way that satisfies both parties. You will be able to develop a more realistic view of what the outcomes may be and what offers are reasonable. You are not just thinking about your own agenda but trying to understand what is important to the other party so you can design a win-win solution.

Start the discussion with the things you agree upon. Good agreements focus on both parties' interests, rather than their positions. It is always ideal to aim for an agreement where both parties feel satisfied. Of course, that cannot always happen but learn to discern the difference between battles and wars. Know what is really important to you and when it is important to negotiate a better working relationship, especially with key stakeholders. Be clear on your goals and try to understand their goals.

ASSERTIVE COMMUNICATION

To negotiate effectively, you need to communicate assertively and clearly so there is no ambiguity, your voice is heard, and you demonstrate confidence. Communicating assertively tells people where you stand, which ultimately improves relationships. Many women don't fully understand what it means to be assertive. Many of them were taught in childhood to be nurturing and supportive. They find it difficult to voice their own opinion, especially if it is in opposition to someone else's. Some women don't want to express disagreement because they are afraid they will upset others or create conflict.

---

[5] Fischer, R., Ury, W., & Patton, B. (1981). Getting to yes. *Negotiating Agreement Without Giving in (traduction française, 1982: Comment réussir une négociation)*. Paris: Seuil.

They don't want to be perceived as domineering or aggressive. But assertive women share their opinions while being sensitive to other people's ideas. This is different from aggressive people who ignore other people's ideas and passive people who don't share their opinions or ideas.

Women often have good and valid reasons why they have learned to be unassertive. A lot of it stems back to self-sabotaging beliefs, or fear of what might happen if they are assertive. An example of such a belief is, "It is uncaring, rude and selfish to say what you want." Another one is, "If I assert myself, I will upset the other person and ruin our relationship." Or still another is, "I will be embarrassed if I say what I think and nobody cares or listens to me."

Many women mistake being non-assertive or passive with being polite. Being a martyr or not advocating for yourself is not an indication of politeness; it is powerless, lacks courage, is disingenuous, and it allows others to violate your rights. You cannot achieve your vision and fulfill your passion if you don't speak up for what you believe. This is a quandary that many women face.

It is important to recognize the difference between passive, assertive, and aggressive communication styles. Being able to identify the verbal and nonverbal characteristics is a good first step to changing the way you communicate.

Still, many women think that assertiveness is the same as being aggressive. There are very important distinctions between stating your opinion assertively and stating your opinion aggressively. A lot of it has to do with attitude and delivery. When stating your opinion, the choice of words, the tone that you use, and your body language should not be confrontational. These are the nonverbal cues (discussed earlier) that are learned and often unconscious. If we are unaware of them, we may not be communicating effectively.

Sometimes women sabotage their assertiveness by saying what they think but sending inconsistent nonverbal cues that contradict their conviction. They don't make eye contact, they slouch, they play with their hair or nails, or they shuffle their feet—all of which detracts from the message and tells the listener that you really don't believe what you are saying, so people will not take you seriously. In fact, this can be even more serious since inconsistency may be interpreted as misleading or duplicitous, or at best, confusing and wishy-washy.

Take caution, as you learn to assert yourself. There are times where the pendulum can swing to the other side. If you are not careful, you could become aggressive in a way that shows a lack of respect for other individual's views or abilities. There is an optimum balance, but it requires awareness and practice. This is a great topic to work on with your Advocacy Circle since chances are, everyone can benefit from being aware of the differences.

EXERCISE—FOCUSING ON AN ASSERTIVE COMMUNICATION STYLE

Part A: Know the difference between assertive, passive, and aggressive. Review how you would behave when you are assertive in the left-hand column of the following table. This is the optimum way of communicating. If you are not behaving as an assertive person, you are acting either passively or aggressively. Fill in how your behavior or communication would change in those instances and then compare it to the suggestions on the answer key.

When I am an assertive, I	When I am a passive, I	When I am aggressive, I
Negotiate for an *I win—you win* solution		
Generally confident		
Give compliments freely and genuinely when appropriate		
Am respected by others		
Demonstrate my values and respect for other's opinions		
Ask for help when needed		
Admit to mistakes and develop a plan to fix them		
Speak appropriately open		
Express anger appropriately		
Use a conversational tone		
Give criticism in a constructive manner		
Receive criticism		
Participate in the group		
Make eye contact		
Facial expression appropriately matches content		
Relax in an open stance		
Keep to the facts and stay on point		
Am aware of other's feelings		
Reach goal without harming others		

Part B: Rate Your Situational Assertiveness

It can be difficult to know how assertive you are since you may behave assertively in some situations, but not in others. Part B of this exercise can help you determine how assertive you are in different situations. Down the left side are the different situations that require assertiveness from Part A. Across the top are different groups of people. Work across cell by cell and rate each combination of situations and groups of people from a scale of 0 to 10. A rating of "10" means you have no problem asserting yourself where a rating of "0" means you cannot assert yourself at all. Then, answer the questions below.

	Female friend	Male friend	Female boss	Male boss	Female colleague	Male colleague	Waitress or salesperson
Negotiate for an I win—you win solution							
Generally confident							
Gives compliments freely and genuinely when appropriate							
Respected by others							
Demonstrate you value others opinions							
Ask for help when needed							
Admit to mistakes and develop plan to fix							
Speak appropriately open							
Express anger when appropriate							
Use conversational tone							
Gives criticism in a constructive manner							
Receives criticism							
Participate in the group							
Make eye contact							
Facial expression appropriately matches content							
Relax in an open stance							
Keep to the facts and stay on point							
Aware of other's feelings							
Reach goal without harming others							

Are you assertive in most situations?

_____
_____
_____
_____
_____
_____
_____
_____
_____

In which situations do you need to work on your assertiveness skills?

_____
_____
_____
_____
_____
_____
_____
_____

Identify a time where you felt you did not communicate as directly as you would have liked. How could you have communicated differently?

_____
_____
_____
_____
_____
_____
_____
_____
_____

Possible Answers for Part A

When I am an assertive, I	When I am a passive, I	When I am aggressive, I
Negotiate for an *I win—you win* solution	Negotiation results in a *you win—I lose* solution	Negotiate for a *I win—you lose* solution
Generally confident	Low confidence	Low confidence or exaggerated confidence
Give compliments freely and genuinely when appropriate	Uncomfortable giving compliments or over-complimentary	Never give compliments
Respected by others	No respect by others	No respect by others
Demonstrate you values others opinions	Demonstrate you values self less than others	Demonstrate you values self more than others
Ask for help when needed	Afraid to ask for help	Afraid to ask for help

When I am an assertive, I	When I am a passive, I	When I am aggressive, I
Admit to mistake and develop plan to fix	Do not admit to mistake, blame others, or inappropriately take blame for everything with no plan to fix	Do not admit to mistake and blame others with no plan to fix
Speak appropriately open	Afraid to speak even when asked	Interrupt others—you have your own agenda
Express anger when appropriately	Never display anger	Display anger inappropriately, sometimes to gain attention
Use conversational tone	Speak softly—can't be heard	Speak loudly and belligerently
Give criticism in a constructive	Do not give criticism even if it could be helpful	Critical in a demeaning way that demotivates
Receive criticism	Cry and accept the fact of failure	Attack back and point the finger at others
Participate in the group	Move away from the group	Insistent and control the group
Make eye contact	Avoid eye contact	Glare at others
Facial expression appropriately matches content	Little facial expression	Intimidate through facial expression
Relax in an open stance	Slouch, play with hair, or other nervous twitch	Stand rigidly, crossing arms, or violate other's personal space
Keep to the facts and stays on point	Agree with others despite own objections	Uncompromising, only aware of own ideas
Aware of other's feelings	Hurt self to avoid hurting others	Antagonistic and hurt other
Reach goal without harming others	Do not reach goals	Reach goals but may cause harm and even future obstacles to reach goals

CONCLUSION

Regan is a domestic violence victim. She had been literally mute for five years and became so one week after she had asked her husband if she could get involved with the family's financial planning. I find the psychological connection fascinating—she literally (and figuratively) could not speak for herself. As an advocate for rape victims, I have learned that offenders become the most violent when their victims assert personal power, so I probed to find out what happened. Eventually she conceded and told me that her husband told her that she was stupid and would never understand. When she disagreed he put her through a wall.

I asked Regan why she didn't leave him. She had her masters so she was educated and she also made her own income as a manager in a corporation. Her response was stunning. She said that although she earned money, he had always managed it and she did not know how to take over. It made me sad. She had everything she needed to get out of the relationship but she didn't have the "perceived" ability or confidence to make it happen. He controlled the money and he controlled her. The ending to Regan's story is exciting though. She is no longer with him, and I just learned her divorce became final last month. And oh yes, coincidentally, her voice is coming back.

When women don't engage in their financial lives, many negative things can happen. The outcome may not be as dire as domestic violence, but overall, disengagement leads to disempowerment. Here are a few examples:

- Marion is an 80-year-old woman who I met last year. She was sold a product that left her destitute. She did know enough about finance to ask the right questions when she was sold the product.
- My friend Claudia has her MBA and a job on Wall Street. When she got divorced, she discovered money was missing from the family account. She had not been participating in the household financial decisions and

L. Mattia, *Gender on Wall Street*,
https://doi.org/10.1007/978-3-319-75550-2

her husband moved the funds out of her reach. We have seen this empirically, where money goes missing during a divorce when one partner hasn't been paying attention.

- Nannette is a widow who came to me for advice. She had allowed her husband to choose a single life annuity for his pension distribution, which left her with no income after his death. She didn't understand the pros and cons of the choice at the time, and perhaps her husband did not either, but now she has a big problem.

Any situation that is not healthy or loving, and does support a good life is an opportunity for change. Many times, women choose an unhealthy situation out of financial dependency, because they are afraid, or they lack confidence in their abilities. We can help remove the worry and fear. We can help all women gain the confidence to become empowered using money. We can provide the tools for change. Figure 1 is an illustration of how women's money empowerment can impact women's lives and their ability to choose their life to achieve well-being. Women who learn how to use money as a powerful tool can live life on their terms and they can even change the world.

This is bigger than you and I. It is more important than money. When women are engaged in the financial world, both as leaders and consumers, they tip the scales and improve all women's ability to live life on their terms.

Fig. 1 Women's money empowerment continuum

This is a key reason why it's so important for women to become financial leaders and advisors; so they can encourage other women to become financially engaged and empowered.

This book is a call to all female financial professionals (and those considering the call) to become consciously engaged in your career and claim your financial leadership position. Be an advocate for women at all stages—both career women or not. Become a leader in shaping the financial industry so it is comfortable and safe for all women to pursue a career in finance or simply become engaged in their own financial lives.

We are in the fifth wave of the women's movement and our mission is to help all women gain control over their money. This is our calling! Helping women to live their lives without worry and on their own terms is a goal for us all to strive for!

INDEX

© The Editor(s) (if applicable) and The Author(s) 2018
L. Mattia, *Gender on Wall Street*,
https://doi.org/10.1007/978-3-319-75550-2